TO FRED 10-15-24

THE EDUCATION OF A STATESMAN

THANK YOU FOR
A GREAT INTERVIEW.

BEST WISHES,

THE EDUCATION OF
A STATESMAN

How Global Leaders Can Repair a Fractured World

JOHN T. SHAW

ROWMAN & LITTLEFIELD
Lanham • Boulder • New York • London

Published by Rowman & Littlefield
An imprint of The Rowman & Littlefield Publishing Group, Inc.
4501 Forbes Boulevard, Suite 200, Lanham, Maryland 20706
www.rowman.com

86-90 Paul Street, London EC2A 4NE

British Library Cataloguing in Publication Information available

Library of Congress Cataloging-in-Publication Data
Names: Shaw, John, 1957- author.
Title: The education of a statesman : how global leaders can repair a fractured world / John T. Shaw.
Description: Lanham, Maryland : Rowman & Littlefield, 2024. | Includes bibliographical references and index.
Identifiers: LCCN 2024015274 (print) | LCCN 2024015275 (ebook) | ISBN 9781538174838 (hardcover) | ISBN 9781538174845 (epub)
Subjects: LCSH: Eliasson, Jan. | Diplomacy. | Diplomats—Sweden—Biography. | Ambassadors—Sweden—Biography.
Classification: LCC DL879.E46 S53 2024 (print) | LCC DL879.E46 (ebook) | DDC 327.4850092 [B]—dc23/eng/20240429
LC record available at https://lccn.loc.gov/2024015274
LC ebook record available at https://lccn.loc.gov/2024015275

♾️™ The paper used in this publication meets the minimum requirements of American National Standard for Information Sciences—Permanence of Paper for Printed Library Materials, ANSI/NISO Z39.48-1992.

CONTENTS

Contents

Acknowledgments

I met Jan Eliasson more than twenty years ago when he was Sweden's ambassador to the United States. I had been searching for an ambassador to study to better understand how high-level diplomacy, especially in Washington, DC, is conducted. At the time, Ambassador Eliasson was one of the stars of Washington's diplomatic corps. I approached him and he agreed to allow me to shadow him and participate in interviews about diplomacy, his career, and his work in Washington. That project culminated in a book published in 2006, *The Ambassador: Inside the Life of a Working Diplomat.*

I kept in touch with Jan over the years and closely followed his time as president of the United Nations General Assembly, Sweden's foreign minister, the UN's special envoy to Darfur, deputy secretary-general of the UN, and chairman of the Stockholm International Peace Research Institute.

I approached Jan in the summer of 2020 and told him about my hope to write a book about the later part of his career, focusing on what he has learned about diplomacy and international affairs. He agreed and we conducted a number of interviews via Zoom and communicated through email. I also interviewed his associates at the UN and in Sweden.

Jan and I agreed that this would be an independent book based on my interpretation of his career.

I would especially like to thank Jan for being open and forthcoming during this project. I would also like to thank his wife, Kerstin Eliasson, for graciously allowing me to take up so much of her husband's time.

A number of Jan's associates and former colleagues have been very helpful, especially Claes Thorson and Monica Lundkvist. Special thanks to Professor Kim-Eric Williams for his helpful summary of Jan's memoir that was written in Swedish.

I would like to extend special thanks to Michael Kerns of Rowman & Littlefield for his enthusiastic support for this project. Michael has been terrific to work with.

I would also like to express my appreciation to my colleagues at the Paul Simon Public Policy Institute.

Many people contributed in various ways to this book. I have especially enjoyed brainstorming with my brother Dave Shaw and my friends Ray Mayfield and Mark Gallagher.

Most of all, I would like to thank my wife, Mindy Steinman, for her unfailing support, steadfast encouragement, and skillful (and exacting!) editing. Mindy brightens every room she enters—and sharpens every sentence she edits.

Author's Note

This book is based on interviews, reporting, and research. It has been enriched by several dozen interviews I had with Jan Eliasson over twenty years. My initial interviews with Jan were conducted between 2003 and 2005 for my book *The Ambassador: Inside the Life of Washington Diplomacy*. That book focused on his tenure as Sweden's ambassador to the United States, but we also spent many hours talking about his love for, and career in, diplomacy.

I began interviewing Jan for *The Education of a Statesman* in the summer of 2020 and then conducted a second round of interviews in the fall of 2023. Additionally, we exchanged countless emails in which we carried on a conversation about diplomacy and international affairs.

JAN ELIASSON CHRONOLOGY

Born September 17, 1940

1957–58: American Field Service program high school exchange student in Decatur, Indiana

1962: Royal Swedish Naval Academy graduation

1965: Master's degree in economics from University of Gothenburg School of Business, Economics and Law

1965: Enter Sweden's Ministry of Foreign Affairs

1970–74: First Secretary, Sweden's embassy to the United States

1980–86: Sweden's United Nations mission, member of the Iran-Iraq mediation team

1982–83: Diplomatic advisor to Prime Minister Olof Palme

1983–87: Director General for Political Affairs in Sweden's Ministry for Foreign Affairs

1988–92: Sweden's ambassador to the UN; Secretary-General's Personal Representative for Iran-Iraq

1991: Chair, UN General Assembly Working Group on Emergency Relief; vice president of the UN Economic and Social Council

1992–94: First UN Under-Secretary-General for Humanitarian Affairs

1994–2000: Sweden's State Secretary for Foreign Affairs

2000–2005: Sweden's ambassador to the United States

September 2005–September 2006: President of UN General Assembly

April–October 2006: Sweden's Foreign Minister

December 2006–June 2008: Special UN Envoy to Darfur

2010: Millennium Development Goals Advocacy Panel

July 2012–December 2016: UN Deputy Secretary-General

2015: The Tällberg Foundation names its Global Leadership Prize after Eliasson

June 2017–June 2022: Chair of the Stockholm International Peace Research Institute (SIPRI)

PART I

SNAPSHOTS OF STATESMANSHIP

CHAPTER 1

Statecraft, Stagecraft, Soulcraft

INTERNATIONAL STATESMAN

Jan Eliasson is a rare triple diplomatic threat. He is skilled at bilateral diplomacy, conducted by two nations, as well as multilateral diplomacy, which transpires in larger international settings such as the United Nations. He is also one of the world's most experienced mediators, a specialized niche of diplomacy that seeks first to prevent and if necessary end disputes and find resolutions through impartial negotiation.

Over the decades Eliasson has grown into an international statesman, displaying vision, compassion, courage, effectiveness, and inspiration. He has mastered statecraft, stagecraft, and soulcraft—the substance, theater, and spirit of diplomacy.

He is superb at statecraft, the traditional work of diplomats, which calls for explaining, advocating, negotiating, clashing (if necessary), and conciliating (as much as possible). He prefers concord to contention but knows there are times for each. "Diplomacy is not always about agreeing. Sometimes it's about being able to express disagreements in a clear and constructive way." He knows when to press hard and when to ease up. "In diplomacy, it's important to have a light touch. When you're always delivering a heavy message, people get tired of you."

Eliasson excels at diplomatic theater—stagecraft—where presentation and dramatic effect are paramount. He understands the importance of stories, gestures, and symbols. "You have to have stories, vivid examples. That's what people remember and that's what inspires them: stories."

3

He is convinced that diplomacy also needs soulcraft—a spiritual dimension to open minds, move people, and lift spirits. "As diplomats we need to dig deeper, to touch people's hearts. We need to inspire and give hope. There is too much fear in the world."

Eliasson is the ultimate inside-outside diplomat, able to maneuver and negotiate behind the scenes and skilled at public presentation and explanation. He understands how governments and international organizations work and the best way to exert influence. "He has a finger-tip feeling for timing," says a former aide. "He never forces things."

STATECRAFT

For Jan Eliasson, March 15, 2006, was a day that most diplomats dream about but never experience. Months of tense, arduous, high-stakes diplomacy is about to culminate with the UN's approval of one of the major initiatives of his long and distinguished career.

As president of the United Nations General Assembly, Eliasson is presiding over the chamber as delegates vote to create a new Human Rights Council. This council is designed to promote and defend human rights around the world. Once in place, and operating effectively, Eliasson is convinced that it will help save thousands of lives, stabilize societies, and bring renewed respect to the UN. This is the dream of a diplomat: to transform an idea into an institution that will make a tangible contribution to the world, in this case to champion human rights.

The Human Rights Council is set to replace the six-decade-old Commission on Human Rights that has been uniformly dismissed and derided for years. Secretary-General Kofi Annan proposed the outlines of the new council two years earlier but left it to Eliasson to give it substance, structure, and life.

As the vote nears, Eliasson sits at the president's elevated green marble desk in front of the UN emblem on a gold background, framed by three-foot-tall shields. Dressed in a dark suit, red tie, and pocket square, Eliasson gazes out at the cavernous hall with tired, hopeful, and wary eyes. He wants to make sure there are no surprises, unexpected delays, or procedural complications. If the General Assembly is, as Eliasson describes, a Cathedral of Peace, the president's desk is its high altar. Eliasson has the best seat in the hall for the coming vote.

The vote is the culmination of five months of difficult diplomacy that has required all of Eliasson's considerable planning, drafting, negotiating, and lobbying skills. He will later observe that creating the Human Rights Council was one of the most daunting challenges of his diplomatic career. He has had to organize, conduct, and repeatedly explain an extraordinarily complex set of ideas involving nearly two hundred countries and thousands of diplomats. The Human Rights Council will be an intricate entity with scores of new procedures and processes. To pull it together and close the deal, he has studied history, consulted with advocates and opponents, and fine-tuned proposals in several languages. He has made dozens of compromises, but also decided when he could compromise no further.

Eliasson had hoped to receive the go-ahead for the Human Rights Council by unanimous consent, as is the case with most UN resolutions. However, opponents of his proposal demanded a formal vote. Eliasson decided to move forward, fully aware that the United States, then the most powerful nation in the UN, would publicly oppose his plan. The American vote in opposition was certain to generate controversy and possibly recriminations. But Eliasson decided there was nothing to be gained by further negotiations. With his keenly developed sense of timing, he believed that delay and additional talks would be counterproductive.

"Today we stand ready to witness a new beginning," he tells the assembled diplomats. "We have now reached a decisive moment, both for the promotion and protection of human rights and for effective multilateralism and the standing of the United Nations as a whole." The package under consideration, he says, is the result of "our common combined effort, intellect, and aspirations."[1]

When the question is called, Eliasson's resolution prevails on a 170 to 4 vote. The United States, Israel, Marshall Islands, and Palau are the only countries that vote against it. Venezuela, Iran, and Belarus abstain.

After gaveling acknowledgment of the resolution's passage, Eliasson leans back in his chair, takes a deep breath, and basks in the moment, taking in the applause. This is the culmination of hard, complicated, and emotionally charged diplomacy. It is a moment of joy, accomplishment, and hope for the veteran diplomat. However, Eliasson's thinking almost immediately shifts to the future challenges for the council: the crucial votes on membership, its first meeting in Geneva, and the work it must actually do to make the world a safer and better place for everyone.

STAGECRAFT

The traditional function of a diplomat is to negotiate with other diplomats. Pinstripes, carefully crafted communiques, and elegant conference rooms have been the symbols of this world. But diplomacy has changed. Diplomats still negotiate, and the good ones do it very well. However, modern diplomats also explain, inspire, and challenge—they tell stories and use symbols to explain complex matters and spur action.

And so it is that in December 2011, Jan Eliasson, one of Sweden's preeminent diplomats, has returned to his hometown of Gothenburg to tell the story of the global water and sanitation crisis. His outlet is a TED Talk at the University of Gothenburg.

Dapper and distinguished in a dark suit, lavender shirt, striped tie, and pocket square, Eliasson stands on a lighted stage, a pitcher and full glass of water on a table to his right. At first glance, it seems the liquid has been placed there to provide refreshment for the speaker. However, for Eliasson it is a device that helps frame his story. During his fifteen-minute presentation, he lifts the glass of water and taps it three times with his left hand, his wedding band making it ring. "Water is life. Water and sanitation is survival for billions of people around the world. And water is a growing reason for conflict around the world." He then adds that water can serve as a "catalyst for cooperation rather than for conflict."

Eliasson wants to make the water crisis as tangible and specific as possible and so he tells a story. "I'll take you on a helicopter ride. A helicopter is not bad for seeing things. You can see everything very clearly from a glass bubble," he says, now transporting his audience from this prosperous city in western Sweden into the roiling, boiling tragedy that was Darfur in 2007. He describes a trip there as the UN special envoy, flying from Al-Fashir, Sudan, to a village in the north. He recalls looking out the window and being captivated by the sand encroaching on grass. "I never thought I would see desertification with my own eyes. But I did."

Upon landing, Eliasson and his team walked down mostly empty streets, past a market in which the only product on offer was onions. Eliasson then approached a group of women moaning and chanting. He asked his interpreter what they were saying. "Water, water. We need water. We need water." He was told this village once had two wells. However, one had been poisoned by the attacking Janjaweed militia and the other dried up. Now the villagers—primarily women and girls—had to walk forty minutes in each direction in the dusty, scorching heat to get poor quality water. This impure water would soon cause sickness and death in the village as scores of children developed "gray skin and empty eyes" and then slowly perished.

Standing before this rapt audience in Gothenburg, Eliasson lifts the glass of water. "This glass of water is a luxury, a dream for 885 million people around the world," he says. About 2.5 billion people—nearly a quarter of humanity—lack adequate sanitation which, Eliasson explains, "is a euphemism for toilets." He adds that nearly 4,000 children under the age of five die every day due to diseases linked to dehydration. A global effort is needed, he says, to address the scarcity of clean water and sanitation. This will ameliorate other problems including child mortality, maternal health, gender inequality, extreme poverty, and poor education. "In today's world, everything is related. There is no peace without development. There is no development without peace. And there is neither peace nor development without respect for human rights—and the right to water is a human right."

"Water touches everything. It is life itself," Eliasson says. The UN should work with regional organizations such as the European Union, the African Union, individual countries, businesses, and civil society such as schools, churches, universities, and advocacy groups to tackle and solve the water and sanitation crises.[2]

Eliasson decided to concentrate on the "practical and concrete" issues of water and sanitation when he returned to Sweden after eighteen months in Darfur. He helped launch WaterAid Sweden, which champions clean water globally. He also became an official UN advocate for the

Millennium Development Goals, which focused on ending poverty. One of the goals specifically urged action on water and sanitation.

Eliasson believes diplomats must explain the world clearly and truthfully but also suggest solutions and provide hope. "In diplomacy, there is too much, 'no comment.' Foreign policy must be part of a lively political debate. We have to explain what we are doing."

SOULCRAFT

It is October 2015 and Jan Eliasson has decided to make good on his decade-long aspiration to marry the mystical musings of Dag Hammarskjöld, the legendary UN secretary-general from Sweden, with some of the world's finest classical music. Eliasson took time from his hectic schedule as deputy secretary-general to help organize and preside over a recital called "Markings and Music" as part of the UN's seventieth anniversary celebration. The evening features readings by Eliasson from Hammarskjöld's book *Markings*, published two years after his 1961 death, and musical interludes by Swedish pianist Per Tengstrand, who plays selections from Chopin, Beethoven, and Bach.

In opening remarks, Eliasson says that he conceived of the event when he was president of the UN General Assembly. However, the pressing business of also serving as Sweden's foreign minister made it impossible to schedule at the time.

Tonight's recital is in the Economic and Social Council Chamber, which was a gift from Sweden to the UN. Designed by the Swedish architect Sven Markelius in the 1950s, the chamber's main floor comprises desks and chairs placed in a horseshoe shape. One wall—a floor-to-ceiling curtain designed with interlocking orange and white triangles meant to symbolize dialogue—is the room's focal point. The ceiling of the elegant conference room appears unfinished; the air vents are intentionally left exposed to remind people that the UN's work is never complete.

The evening alternates between selections from *Markings*, commentary by Eliasson, and Tengstrand's music. When he was secretary-general, Hammarskjöld hosted concerts in the General Assembly Hall to inspire a connection between music and diplomacy. He especially enjoyed listening to Beethoven's "Ode to Joy" on UN Day.

Eliasson describes Hammarskjöld as a man of action and culture, a Swedish technocrat who emerged as a surprise candidate to become secretary-general and, ultimately, a venerated global statesman. He pioneered preventive diplomacy, peacekeeping, and the ethos of international civil service in which national identity coexists with commitment to internationalism and the UN Charter. Eliasson depicts Hammarskjöld as a man of reflection and action with a deep spirituality. He recalls that when Sweden learned that Hammarskjöld was killed when his plane crashed in 1961, the country went "absolutely numb." Eliasson was a young naval cadet at the time and was deeply shaken by the news of the secretary-general's death. "This was the first time I said to myself, 'I should work at the United Nations.'"

Eliasson says that when he first read *Markings* as a young man, the meditations had little impact. Now they inspire and guide him. And he finds them especially powerful when coupled with classical music. The combination of music and mystical musings encourages people to take "the long view" of problems and challenges.

He reads aloud from the book: "Never measure the height of a mountain until you have reached the top. Then you will see how low it was."

He carefully reads from Hammarskjöld's musing on the importance of language. "Respect for the word is the first commandment in the discipline by which a man can be educated to maturity—intellectual, emotional, and moral. Respect for the word—to employ it with scrupulous care and incorruptible heartfelt love of truth—is essential if there is to be any growth in a society or in the human race. To misuse the word is to show contempt for man. It undermines the bridges and poisons the wells. It causes Man to regress down the long path of his evolution." This prompts Eliasson to elaborate on diplomacy: "We should collect words. It's our most important tool. We should use them to improve the lives of others. Diplomacy, to some, is vagueness. To me, it's about clarity."

He continues with Hammarskjöld's meditation on the need to "free us from all fear." This elicits Eliasson's reflection that there is too much fear in the world and that it is used by those who want to intimidate and dominate. Eliasson has a different aspiration. "We need to mobilize all the good forces we have and stand up for another narrative of hope and compassion. It's a very important message in today's world."[3]

Reflecting on this recital several years later, Eliasson says many of the diplomats in attendance told him they relished the merging of music and mysticism, and appreciated, in a new way, the spiritual dimension of their work. "I think art and culture and music can play a very important role in reminding ourselves what is universal, and it can also reach our hearts. Diplomacy is not about shaking hands, diplomacy is touching the hearts," Eliasson declares.

THE DIPLOMAT FROM CENTRAL CASTING

Jan Eliasson is one of the most accomplished diplomats of his generation. He steadily ascended to the top tier of global diplomacy over a half century, taking on increasingly challenging assignments and performing them skillfully and with flair. Smart and suave, Eliasson looks like James Bond of the Roger Moore variety. He is a classically trained diplomat who speaks four languages, has mastered the art of negotiation, can craft a communique, deliver a toast, work a room, hold his own on the dance floor, and broker a peace agreement. One could easily imagine Eliasson operating as successfully at the Congress of Vienna in 1815 or the Paris Peace talks of 1919 as he did at the Iran nuclear negotiations of 2015. Charming and charismatic, he is also substantive and detail-oriented. Now in his eighties, he is more idealistic than many in their twenties, but it is an idealism that has been tested and tempered by war zones, refugee camps, brass-knuckled negotiations, grueling international travel, and bureaucratic obstinacy.

Eliasson prefers persuasion in which the command of facts and the precise use of language brings about resolution. However, he can be forceful, relentless, and even unyielding, deploying sharp elbows when appropriate. "I am not a person who enjoys a conflict," he says. "But sometimes I land in confrontation. I don't enjoy it, but I can do it. I can be very, very firm."

He is a complicated, multilayered man. Kind, considerate, and sentimental, yet ambitious, driven, and self-promotional. Extroverted and affable, he has been likened to an American politician by both his champions and his critics. He is a shrewd judge of character and has a keen eye for idiosyncrasies, absurdities, and peccadilloes. He notices everything; he forgets nothing. It may not be a coincidence that he collects magnifying glasses. He reads people like an experienced intelligence officer and finds the best way to engage them. He can discuss American and global politics, world history, international relations, sports, travel, literature, music, film, and TV. When he was Sweden's ambassador in Washington, he charmed Condoleezza Rice with discussions about classical music and piano recitals. He bantered with Colin Powell about Volvos and ABBA. Eliasson controls and channels his intensity. "I'm probably more temperamental than I seem. I have a temper, but I don't get irritated in public."

Well-known and highly regarded in American, European, and global diplomatic circles, he has been called a "diplomatic superstar" and "one of the world's most remarkable diplomats." Less charitable descriptions emanate from those whom he has battled, such as former American ambassador to the UN, John Bolton, who derided him as a grandstander.

Eliasson is resilient, undaunted, and relishes his profession. "Being a diplomat is my first identity," he says. "I have great respect for the art of diplomacy. I love the work. I love the trade. It's the most civilized way to solve conflicts." He believes diplomats, through the skillful use of language, can fix problems, ease suffering, and provide hope. "Words— the right words—can save lives," he says, citing a time when his mediation team in Sudan abandoned the concept of a "ceasefire" during a dispute and seized on the term "humanitarian corridor." This linguistic adjustment broke a stalemate and allowed delivery of critical supplies to refugees, saving thousands of people from starvation. "Language is the principal working tool for the diplomat," he says. "It can be used to reassure, convince, or coerce. Words may be powerful, ambiguous, or pregnant with violence. There is a saying, 'without language there would be no poetry or war.'"

Eliasson admires successful statesmen, particularly fellow Swedes Raoul Wallenberg, Dag Hammarskjöld, Olof Palme, and Anna Lindh. Wallenberg, the scion of privilege, risked—and ultimately lost—his life saving thousands of Jews during World War II. Hammarskjöld was, almost without dispute, the best UN secretary-general in history and demonstrated how a devoted Swedish civil servant could grow into an international statesman. Palme was a colorful and formidable Swedish prime minister who introduced Eliasson to high-level politics and diplomacy. He changed Eliasson's professional life, catapulting him into the big leagues of international mediation. Anna Lindh was a forceful and tough-minded Swedish foreign minister whom Eliasson worked for, clashed with, and ultimately respected. As it happened, all these Swedish role models met untimely deaths—Lindh and Palme were murdered in Stockholm, while Hammarskjöld was killed in a plane crash under suspicious circumstances. Eliasson, however, is drawn more to their successes than their martyrdom.

Eliasson has been blessed with many years of good health and productive work like his most important mentor, Brian Urquhart. A British and international civil servant who was an under-the-radar UN superstar for four decades, Urquhart was better qualified to be secretary-general than anyone except Hammarskjöld but never got the top job because of the tradition that this position would never go to diplomats from any of the five permanent members of the UN Security Council. Like Eliasson, Urquhart enjoyed a stellar career at the top tier of global diplomacy, one rung below the top of the ladder. He was renowned for his integrity, skill, courage, and calm. Qualities that also describe Eliasson. Urquhart was keenly respected for his hard-headed understanding of practical limitations and constraints and was famous for his irreverence, lack of pretension, and wit, much of it self-deprecating. "Brian Urquhart was a legend and a mentor. I learned so much from him," Eliasson says.

LESSONS FROM A STATESMAN

Eliasson is a polished performer, able to read and capture a room. "Jan can tell the same story over and over and you would think that he is telling it for the first time. But he doesn't do it because it's the easy go to. He does repetition for reinforcement," says a former aide. In his speeches, Eliasson has a ready supply of formulations that are delivered with the freshness of a first-time telling.

"You must have both roots and wings," he tells students. "You must know where you came from but also be adventurous and see the world.

Learn from the past, live intensely in the present, and have dreams and aspirations for the future." He also urges students to combine passion and compassion. "Without passion, nothing happens. Without compassion, the wrong things happen," he declares. When speaking about climate and the environment he says, "In life, we all must have a Plan B. But in our world, there is no Planet B."

A lifelong learner who has never grown stale, Eliasson's curiosity was ignited as a boy and has never waned. His interests range from the lofty to the prosaic. He can speak as easily about American movies as Iranian carpets, or European football and African folk rituals. In the midst of a highly charged and contentious mediation during the Iran-Iraq war, he stayed up nearly all night to watch the 1989 US Open men's tennis final between fellow Swede, Mats Wilander, and Ivan Lendl. "I was exhausted the next day, but it was worth it," he says with a smile decades later. "I told my Iranian and Iraqi counterparts that Swedes are good at tennis."

If Eliasson were on a plane and was handed a stack of reading material including the daily UN news digest, a foreign policy journal, and an international relations textbook, he would read them in that order. He would devour the news summary, peruse the foreign policy journal, and skim the textbook. He prefers the tangible to the theoretical. But before reading anything, Eliasson would first circulate through the cabin to see if he knew, and wanted to speak to, any of the other passengers.

"Jan Eliasson is an extreme, extreme, extrovert," says a former aide. He draws energy from interacting with people, even those he hardly knows. A Swedish professor recalls taking a taxi to the Stockholm airport with Eliasson to discuss a research project, but Eliasson spent much of the ride bantering with the driver about sports. "He just can't help himself," the professor recalled with a laugh. Eliasson is a relentless and instinctive networker. He meets people easily, remembers names and faces, keeps in touch, and connects them to others.

Eliasson knows everyone in global diplomacy and American politics. He worked with more than half of the UN secretaries-general: Kurt Waldheim, Javier Pérez de Cuéllar, Boutros Boutros-Ghali, Kofi Annan, Ban Ki-moon, and António Guterres. He has interacted with a half dozen American presidents: Bill Clinton, George W. Bush, Barack

Obama, Donald Trump, and Joe Biden. He has known almost every consequential American diplomat over the last half century including Henry Kissinger, George Shultz, Tom Pickering, Strobe Talbott, Condoleezza Rice, Colin Powell, Samantha Power, Susan Rice, Brent Scowcroft, Steve Hadley, William Burns, Nicholas Burns, Madeleine Albright, and Antony Blinken. During his ambassadorship in Washington, Eliasson was on a first-name basis with the presidents of all the major think tanks and most of the Supreme Court justices, many of whom often attended his embassy parties. Sandra Day O'Connor and Martin Ginsberg, the husband of Justice Ruth Bader Ginsberg, prepared a farewell luncheon for Jan and Kerstin Eliasson at the Supreme Court. Before the lunch, Eliasson had a private conversation with Swedish American Chief Justice William Rehnquist, a relationship Eliasson cultivated and enjoyed.

STUDYING A STATESMAN

In the pages that follow we will learn about Jan Eliasson's rise through the ranks, becoming one of Sweden's most accomplished diplomats in the history of a foreign service with a stellar international reputation. We will pay particular attention to his strong relationships with UN and American diplomats, which have been critical to his career. We will also carefully consider his deep and wide experiences at the United Nations. These have been profoundly important to his professional development and worldview. We will closely examine diplomatic episodes from the later stages of his career, including his work on human rights, Darfur, the Sustainable Development Goals, and his quest to build a culture of prevention. We will then look at his career from a wider lens to understand statesmanship and how it can help repair the tattered international rules-based order—the array of organizations, alliances, and procedures, primarily created in the aftermath of World War II, including the UN, World Bank, International Monetary Fund, European Union, and NATO.

As an international statesman, Eliasson has seen a lot, learned from his experiences, and has much to teach us. Even though he is now officially retired, he remains plugged into important issues and retains high-level contacts across the world. An esteemed elder in global affairs,

Eliasson keeps in touch with diplomats he has mentored who are now rising through the ranks. They always return his phone calls.

Eliasson has a remarkable ability to see around corners, to understand how issues connect, and to predict what policies will work and which will fail. He is not omniscient, but he is savvy and experienced. Very little surprises him and he has considerable wisdom to impart. "They don't make diplomats like Jan Eliasson anymore," says a former aide. "He can capture people's interests and capture their imagination."

As the pages that follow will show, Eliasson has learned critical truths and is skilled at describing them to those who should hear them.

He knows that the international system is complex and essential but also fragile, especially now as it is being assailed by restless progressives, fiery populists, and impatient publics. "The liberal international order has worked effectively for seventy-five years but is now under serious strain. It must deliver results," he says.

He believes the United Nations' successes are largely overlooked and its failures are magnified. But Eliasson realizes that lamenting this unfairness is pointless and self-indulgent. The UN must show it can improve lives and offer a compelling narrative that explains its accomplishments. While flawed, the UN must be reformed rather than started anew. "If we closed the UN today, we would have to start all over and we would probably not do as good the second time," he says. He believes the UN Charter, the global body's constitution, is a document of extraordinary vision, power, and practicality. It can, if adhered to, held build a better world.

He knows that it is easier to destroy than to create. It took years and thousands of hours of intricate diplomacy to fashion the Iranian nuclear agreement and only several reckless minutes by an American president to damage it, perhaps beyond repair.

He believes that a broad and comprehensive definition of security is necessary. It must embrace the military and politics but also economics, human rights, climate, education, and sustainable development. He has learned that diplomacy is becoming more difficult because of social media, cable TV, instant communication, proxy wars, and ethnic tensions. Yet it is more important now than ever before.

He knows that crisis prevention is far preferable to crisis response—even though it is rarely rewarded in the political world. "We need to be there when the arsonist reaches for the match, not when the building has been burned down," he pleads.

He knows that to successfully battle nationalists and populists it is essential to out-prepare them, hold your ground, keep your cool, and tell a compelling story. He has learned that diplomacy is best conducted with clear purpose, steel nerves, and a soft touch. "You can be serious and still have a light side." Different diplomatic contexts require different approaches, but it is almost always best to begin with persuasion. Conciliation is essential but that sometimes threats—which he calls "drums in the distance"—can be useful.

He believes there is an urgent need to narrow the gap between the world that is and the world that should be. Timing is everything, and the right proposals offered at the wrong time don't work. He has learned that in diplomacy, as in life, persistence, even relentless persistence, is essential. "Giving up," Eliasson often says, "is undignified. There is always a way."

Drawing from these broad convictions and thousands of specific events, negotiations, and interactions, Eliasson offers a critical perspective on how the global community can tackle the staggering array of problems that have accumulated at our doorstep. These are lessons we must all learn, and especially today's global leaders, if we are to avert catastrophe and a total breakdown of cooperation.

TIME OF DANGER

Eliasson's wisdom comes at an urgent time in global affairs. During his first State of the Union Address more than half a century ago, President John F. Kennedy warned Americans that they were facing "an hour of national peril," that "we shall have to test anew whether a nation organized and governed such as ours can endure," and that "each day we draw near the hour of maximum danger."[4]

Eliasson believes that Kennedy's stark warning to Americans in 1961 is grimly relevant to the international order now. That system of organizations, alliances, and procedures that was constructed after World War II is reaching its hour of maximum danger. It faces cascading and connected threats: the brutal pandemic, worsening climate change, growing inequalities, deepening economic insecurity, exploding digital vulnerabilities, empowered demagogues, tidal waves of refugees, faltering institutions, and proliferating weapons of mass destruction. Most troubling at this time of mounting danger—international solidarity is crumbling and national governments are consumed by internal problems.

Jan Eliasson is neither a miracle worker nor a magician, but he is a wise man who can help us chart a better way. Let us watch and learn from one of the most skilled diplomats of our time.

We will see his rise to the pinnacle of global diplomacy and consider the skills he developed, the contacts he made, and the lessons he learned. What qualities are necessary to be a diplomatic superstar and at what personal costs to one's family and friendships? We will learn about the United Nations from a man who has served there as an ambassador, special envoy, under secretary-general, president of the General Assembly, and deputy secretary-general—and arguably knows more about it than anyone else living. What does the UN do well? What are its failings? How can it be improved?

We will see Eliasson battle to create the UN Human Rights Council and champion another critical human rights initiative, Human Rights Up Front. How can human rights, first enshrined in the UN Universal Declaration of Human Rights in 1948, be better advanced and protected around the world?

We will see him in Darfur trying, and failing, to end a horrific civil war and we will see him struggling to persuade the Security Council to end the war in Syria. How does the clash of local, regional, and global actors create maximum suffering and chaos in war zones?

We will see Eliasson work to complement the Paris Climate Accords of 2015 with a lesser known, but critical, companion initiative called the Sustainable Development Goals. Eliasson calls this program a "tool box to save the world." How do the SDGs create a path to reduce poverty, boost education, reduce inequality, preserve the environment, and enforce justice?

We will see him back in Sweden using his reputation as a global elder to rebuild a decaying international system by careful argument and vivid stories. He will ponder how to teach students and young diplomats to tackle daunting problems with passion and skill; how to collect and deploy synonyms to design agreements to save lives. And he will share his theory of the art, and necessity, of the 45-second conversation in diplomacy.

We will learn the central lessons that Eliasson has absorbed during his storied and consequential career. And we will ask for his best wisdom on forging the way to a better future.

On a personal note, I have known Jan Eliasson for twenty years. In 2006 I wrote *The Ambassador: Inside the Life a Working Diplomat* about his tenure as Sweden's ambassador to the United States. I have followed his career since then and conducted more than a dozen extensive interviews and substantial email correspondence with him in preparation for *The Education of a Statesman.*

This book is my interpretation of the lessons that can be learned from the career of one of the finest diplomats of our generation.

PART II

DIPLOMATIC LIFE

Rising through the Ranks

HUMBLE BEGINNINGS

Jan Kenneth Eliasson was born September 17, 1940, into a working-class family in Gothenburg, Sweden. His father, John, was a metal worker and, later, a taxi driver. His mother, Karin, was a seamstress. For the first decade of his life, Jan lived a one-bedroom home with his parents and his younger brother, Roger.

As he looks back on his youth, Eliasson does not emphasize privation or struggle, but purpose and determination. His parents were quite different from each other. He describes his father as "tough as nails. He was a leader. He was very measured, cool." His mother was a woman of warmth. "She was kindness personified."

John was challenging and tough-minded and dreamed of his oldest son as a politician. As the adult Jan rose rapidly up the ranks of Swedish diplomacy, his father reminded him to be modest, humble, and aware that circumstances can change. He told his son that he was living with "borrowed feathers"—a phrase that referred to both temporary offices and titles as well as to fleeting fame.

Jan's brother, Roger, is four and a half years younger; the two share a friendship and a rivalry. Jan's focus on diplomacy led him to become one of the best diplomats of his generation. Roger's business acumen led him to become one of Sweden's most successful executives.

As a child Jan was a gifted student and skilled athlete. Curious about the world from a young age, he loved to read and would sometimes slip under his covers at night with a flashlight. He enjoyed the books of Karl May, a German novelist of the American West, and devoured books about cowboys.

Jan was a confident and outgoing boy who was skilled in languages. In addition to his native Swedish, he became fluent in English, German, and French and could read Latin. He was an extrovert who enjoyed people and remembered their names and their stories. "If your father was a metal worker and your mother was a seamstress, you recognize your parents in everybody," he says.

Eliasson was selected for an American Field Service program to spend a high school year in the United States, which became a defining life event. He left his home in western Sweden in the summer of 1957 for Rotterdam, where he joined hundreds of other European exchange students for the boat journey to the United States. As the ship neared America, Eliasson recalls waking in the predawn darkness to watch the Statue of Liberty come into view. He still recites from memory the inscription on the statue: "Give me your tired, your poor, your huddled masses yearning to breathe free." He finds the words profound, inspirational, and instructive, a reminder of the kind of world he still wants to help build.

Eliasson lived with Harry and Mildred Hebble, and their two sons, Harry and John, in Decatur, Indiana. Mr. Hebble was an optician who was interested in world affairs and active in the local Democratic Party. Eliasson remembers devouring the Sunday *New York Times* when it was delivered to the Hebble home. He became keenly interested in American politics, especially in a young Democratic senator, John F. Kennedy, who was preparing to run for president. Eliasson persuaded his "American dad" to invite Kennedy to speak at the Jefferson-Jackson dinner event in Indianapolis rather than the more obvious choice, Senator Estes Kefauver, who had been the Democratic vice-presidential candidate in 1956. Happily, Kennedy accepted and Eliasson met him and received an autograph he treasures to this day. It's inscribed, "Hope you enjoy your stay. John Kennedy."

Eliasson was active in school and sports in Decatur and found almost everything about the United States interesting. He had an influential debate coach, Dean Dorwin, who taught him speaking techniques that Eliasson used throughout his diplomatic career. He concluded his year in America with a bus trip to fourteen states with several dozen other AFS students. During one leg of the journey, Jan joined a political discussion between Greek and Turkish girls about the dispute over Cyprus. After listening for a time he suggested offering minority rights to Turkish Cypriots. The girls smiled at his suggested compromise and said he should work at the United Nations one day.

When he returned home to Sweden, his fascination with the United States at first interested, and then exhausted, his parents and brother. Eliasson's year in Indiana ignited a lifelong passion for the United States and a deep curiosity about the outside world. Gothenburg now seemed too small to him.

After completing high school in Sweden, he attended the Royal Swedish Naval Academy and spent three years studying and traveling with the navy. "I had a strong sense of discovery to see new horizons. I wanted some fresh air." He was commissioned a naval officer after being deployed in the Mediterranean and Baltic Sea regions. His naval experience became part of his identify and he refers to it when he describes his love of water, his ability to manage affairs with a stern hand if needed, and his preference for comity rather than contention. "I've been on a happy ship, and I've been on an unhappy ship. I prefer being on a happy ship," he says.

FINDING HIS PROFESSIONAL PASSION

On September 18, 1961, while deployed with the navy in the North Baltic Sea, Eliasson learned that Sweden's legendary civil servant, diplomat, and the secretary-general of the United Nations, Dag Hammarskjöld, had been killed in a plane crash in Africa. Jan was devastated. He deeply admired Hammarskjöld's effective and principled diplomacy on the global stage, including his shrewd and effective actions to ease the 1956 Suez Canal crisis in which Israel, France, and Great Britain seized the canal and went to war with Egypt. Eliasson said that the news of Hammarskjöld's death propelled him to pursue a career in diplomacy and international affairs.

Eliasson earned a master's degree in economics at the University of Gothenburg in 1965. Soon after, his dream was realized when, having passed a rigorous test, he was invited to join Sweden's foreign ministry. He was a member of a class of fifteen young diplomats that autumn, about half of whom would eventually become ambassadors. The Swedish foreign service, once a bastion for the elite, was now opening its doors to a wider group including people like Eliasson from working-class backgrounds. However, even in progressive Sweden, there were only two women in his class.

Sweden's foreign ministry is regarded as one of the most competent and skilled in the world. It has, for generations, produced world-class diplomats who embody and embrace Sweden's respect for international cooperation and devotion to international law and the United Nations. Skilled diplomats and adept diplomacy have allowed Sweden to excel on the global stage.

For his diplomatic training, Eliasson rotated through the foreign ministry's political, trade, and consular sections, followed by six months in the finance ministry. His two-year training concluded with six months at the Organisation for Economic Co-operation and Development in Paris. There, during the summer holidays, he and another junior Swedish diplomat were thrust into a high-level five-day negotiation pertaining to the shipbuilding industry because more senior diplomats were on vacation. They excelled in the talks and were congratulated by several senior ministers and diplomats.

About this time, Eliasson became engaged to, and then married, Kerstin Englesson. She had studied French and economics at Stockholm University and is a highly skilled pianist. Kerstin became one of Sweden's most respected experts on science policy and took the lead in raising their three children, Anna, Emilie, and Johan.

Eliasson's talents made him a potential star and his early career included postings as a junior diplomat in Paris, Bonn, and Washington, where he served for four years from 1970 to 1974. These were contentious years in the US-Swedish relationship. Swedish prime minister Olof Palme sharply criticized the Nixon administration about the war in Vietnam. Palme spoke on Swedish radio just before Christmas 1972 and blasted the Americans for devastating bombing attacks in North Vietnam, which he compared to indiscriminate attacks by the Nazis and Soviets during World War II. President Nixon was furious at Palme and put the Swedish-American diplomatic relationship into deep freeze. At American insistence, for more than a year there was no Swedish ambassador in Washington and no American ambassador serving in Stockholm.

During this time Eliasson continued his work at the Washington embassy as a political analyst and plunged into projects that junior diplomats typically do not get close to. He loved the Swedish ambassador's elegant residence in northwest Washington, and began dreaming of living in the house one day. "I think I wanted to be the ambassador," he recalls with a smile.

IMPORTANT MENTOR

It was during his assignment to Washington in the early 1970s that Eliasson first met Olof Palme in person—a man who would be central to his career. The encounter at the Washington embassy was brief but must have left a distinct impression on Palme. Several years later, in November 1980, Eliasson was surprised by a phone call from Palme, then Sweden's opposition leader, asking him to join his small team of UN mediators searching for a solution to the war between Iran and Iraq. The two men flew the following day from Stockholm to New York for meetings at the United Nations. We will discuss Eliasson's work with Palme on the Iran-Iraq war more fully in the next chapter, but it is critical to consider his relationship with Palme.

Over the next five years, Eliasson traveled frequently with Palme to the Middle East and conferred with him often and intensely about the quest for peace or, at least, a ceasefire between Iran and Iraq. Eliasson served as Prime Minister Palme's diplomatic advisor in 1982 and 1983 and worked with him while serving as the foreign ministry's director-general for political affairs beginning in 1983.

Though Eliasson had several important mentors in the early phase of his diplomatic career, Palme was far and away the most important in his life. Palme was a giant in Swedish public and cultural life. Born in 1927, he was a boy wonder of Swedish and European politics. He was the leader of Sweden's Social Democratic Party from 1969 until his death in 1986. He held a number of ministerial posts, served as prime minister from 1969 to 1976, opposition leader from 1976 to 1982, and again as prime minister from 1982 until his death in 1986.[1]

More important than his longevity in Swedish politics was his intellectual and moral heft. He was widely regarded as a global statesman who carefully and skillfully kept Sweden on an independent path during the Cold War. He sharply criticized the United States over Vietnam and the Soviet Union for its 1968 invasion of Czechoslovakia and its 1979 invasion of Afghanistan. Palme challenged General Francisco Franco's authoritarian rule in Spain and fiercely opposed the apartheid regime in South Africa. A champion of Global South countries, he was the first Western head of government to visit Cuba after Castro came to power. He supported international cooperation, arms control, and the environment.

Eliasson worked closely with Palme for more than five years and found him a captivating and challenging boss who would call him at all hours of the day or night and expect him to leave his home and family on a moment's notice for an overseas trip. His wife, Kerstin, supported her husband's career, giving him the freedom to work long hours and travel frequently, but it no doubt put a strain on their family life.

Eliasson sometimes questioned Palme's combative and defiant style, but observed he could be patient and diplomatic when the moment required. His proximity to Palme prompted him to think about his own diplomatic style, which led him to consider a story from *Aesop's Fables* about the Wind and the Sun. When the competing elements of force and persuasion try to induce a traveler to take off his coat, the Wind's powerful gusts fail but the warm sunshine succeeds. "Thus, the Sun was declared the winner, and ever since then, persuasion has been held in higher esteem than force. Indeed, sunshine of a kind and gentle manner will sooner open a poor man's heart than all the threats and force of blustering authority."[2] Eliasson would cite this fable for decades, often thinking about it during high-stakes diplomatic negotiations.

Palme's assassination in February 1986 in the streets of Stockholm was shattering for Eliasson. His hero, role model, and mentor was gone and Eliasson was briefly adrift. But he regained his footing, pressed ahead, and continued to rise through the ranks of Swedish diplomacy. He served in several key UN jobs in New York in the late 1980s and early 1990s that will be discussed in the next chapter.

DIPLOMACY ON THE HOME FRONT

When he returned to Sweden in 1994, Eliasson took a sabbatical from the foreign ministry to study and teach conflict prevention as a visiting professor at Uppsala University. Later that year he became Sweden's deputy foreign minister, known there as the state secretary for foreign affairs. This is traditionally the highest position a career diplomat can reach. Eliasson served in the post from 1994 to 2000, proudly working from the desk once used by Dag Hammarskjöld when he held the position. Eliasson served under two Swedish foreign ministers, Lena Hjelm-Wallen from 1994 to 1998 and Anna Lindh from 1998 to 2000. Both women were successful politicians who learned the nuances of diplomacy. Hjelm-Wallen was tough-minded and pragmatic. Lindh was a large and charismatic personality who seemed poised to become prime minister. She wanted to advance a bold agenda and charged Eliasson with developing concrete ideas. They collaborated on a proposal to create a culture of prevention, which will be discussed in a subsequent chapter.

Eliasson had a solid relationship with both foreign ministers, but observers noted that there was some tension between Lindh and Eliasson. She may have preferred a deputy who was more of a tidy and efficient administrator rather than an independent voice in the foreign ministry.

Eliasson had become a respected voice in Sweden. In January 1995, on the fiftieth anniversary of the disappearance of Raoul Wallenberg, Eliasson was invited to speak before the Swedish Parliament, an indication of his rising stature. Wallenberg, the Swedish diplomat who helped save tens of thousands of Hungarian Jews during World War II, is a moral giant in Swedish history and for Eliasson to be selected to commemorate him was a singular honor.

Eliasson celebrated Wallenberg's "unfailing moral compass" and inspiring example. "He was one of us, a man who showed that action is possible and necessary. He showed that we do not always need to be prepared or to take deliberate decisions to do what is right. He showed us that we can all rise to the occasion, which can take over and inspire us to superhuman effort. He showed that powerlessness does indeed exist—but it can be overcome by tackling one problem at a time and by always working and planning for a better future, a new sense of fellowship."[3]

AMBASSADOR TO THE UNITED STATES

A new chapter in Eliasson's diplomatic career began in 2000 when he learned that Rolf Ekéus, Sweden's highly regarded ambassador to the United States, planned to step down and return to Sweden. The job was Eliasson's if he wanted it. He did. While it was technically a demotion to move from deputy foreign minister to ambassador, the ambassadorship to the United States is one of the premier jobs in Swedish diplomacy. Eliasson saw the move to Washington as an opportunity to operate on a large stage in a country he knew well. And he would run the embassy; he would be in charge.

Sweden sends its best diplomats to Washington and only the most seasoned and experienced serve as ambassador. Ekéus was a man of substance and depth who was one of the world's leading experts on arms control. A quiet and reserved man, he commanded deep respect in DC. An earlier Swedish ambassador to the United States, Wilhelm Wachtmeister, provided a different model. He served from 1974 to 1989, eventually rising to become the dean of the diplomatic corps in Washington, a designation bestowed on the most senior ambassador in the city. Wachtmeister had a serious career in Swedish diplomacy and was a social lion in Washington, building a vast social network. He often invited senior American policymakers to his parties and tennis court.

Eliasson combined elements of both Ekéus and Wachtmeister. He was a seasoned and substantive diplomat with real expertise in the United Nations and the United States, and he was a formidable social operator.

Eliasson's American expertise was shaped by his Indiana high school year, service as a Swedish diplomat in DC in the 1970s, and extensive work in New York at the UN during the 1980s. He was a veteran diplomat. However, this assignment to Washington would be his first bilateral ambassadorship. Most of Eliasson's previous high-level diplomatic work occurred either within Sweden's foreign ministry or at the UN. This would be his first experience as ambassador to a single country. Eliasson was confident he could make the transition, but he was aware that he needed to master a different type of diplomacy.

Before moving to Washington, he spent part of the summer at his vacation home in Gotland, an island in the Baltic Sea. On a yellow legal notepad, he sketched out his strategy to connect his embassy with the US administration, Congress, the think tank community, business leaders, defense officials, and the Swedish American community. He had a plan and was willing to adjust it as circumstances required.

Eliasson arrived in Washington in the late summer of 2000, just months before the bitterly controversial presidential election between George W. Bush and Al Gore. He developed solid relationships with the outgoing Clinton administration but knew he needed to cultivate wide-ranging relationships with both parties and identify people who might serve in an incoming administration.

Fortunately for Eliasson, Sweden assumed the six-month rotating presidency of the European Union in January 2001. This allowed Eliasson to serve as one of the EU's de facto spokesmen in Washington. He realized this opportunity would give Sweden high-level access to the American government and he intended to seize this opening. "We prepared meticulously," he said. He developed personal relationships with senior members of the new Bush administration, including Secretary of State Colin Powell and National Security Advisor Condoleezza Rice.

Eliasson made what he called a "strategic decision" to offer his embassy as the host of the Washington Opera Ball reception, one of the premier social events in the city. More than six hundred people flocked to the embassy on a glorious June night in 2001 and thrust Sweden into the epicenter of DC social life. The ball helped Eliasson forge important relationships and expand his contacts with political leaders and social luminaries.

In the ensuing years, he actively used the Swedish embassy to host meetings, working lunches, and evening receptions that attracted Washington's "A" list: Supreme Court justices, business and think tank leaders, members of Congress, and their staffers. He approached receptions carefully—selecting the type of event, overseeing the preparation of guest lists, crafting an appropriate toast, and working the room to greet every guest, if only briefly. Here we have Eliasson's theory of diplomacy and the art of the 45-second conversation. He believes that diplomatic receptions provide enough time to connect and exchange information with guests but not to linger or be mired in prolonged discussions. He believes 45 seconds is enough time to make an important and respectful connection—to ask about a spouse or children, discuss recent travel, or preview a coming project or event.

Eliasson is a classic extrovert and drew energy from these events, but he was clear that they were work, not just fun. "I'm always performing, always sending messages, exchanging cards," he said. He endeavored to strike the right tone. He developed easy and productive relationships with Powell and Rice and resumed earlier friendships and professional relationships with senior State Department diplomats including Nicholas Burns, Tom Pickering, Strobe Talbott, William Burns, and Madeleine Albright.

He believed that diplomats from small, nonadversarial nations, like Sweden, would only be listened to if their views and opinions were nuanced, and compelling. They must offer a unique perspective—and Eliasson did. He cultivated journalists who enjoyed interacting with a dashing and experienced diplomat who understood the UN, the United States, and had traveled much of the world. At the prestigious White House Correspondents' dinner, he was invited to sit at the *Newsweek* table. His invitation to the exclusive Gridiron dinner led to a chat with a recently elected young senator from Illinois, Barack Obama.

Eliasson urged his embassy staff to take what he called a mental journey across the Atlantic Ocean and endeavor to see the world from the American perspective. This would help them understand that the United States often did not feel the same respect for international law and multilateral procedures as did smaller, less powerful nations. He also gently urged Americans to think about how the world looked from European eyes. Their continent had been ravaged by two world wars in fairly quick succession and seemed finally to find peace and prosperity only through international cooperation.

Eliasson was in Washington on September 11, 2001. He understood immediately that the world was about to change and suspected that America was about to embark on a fundamentally new path. He sent a sober report to Stockholm. "I said I think this will change the course of history, change the course of American foreign policy. One of my colleagues thought I highly exaggerated." He later told Eliasson that he had been right.

Eliasson constantly looked for ways to connect the United States and Sweden. He was especially protective of the annual White House reception that Sweden cohosted to celebrate the American winners of Nobel Prizes. In the fall of 2001, on the heels of 9/11, the Bush administration considered canceling that year's event. Eliasson worked his contacts relentlessly to keep it on the calendar. He was convinced this annual opportunity to interact with senior White House and administration officials must be preserved at all costs. Allowing the event to lapse, even for one year, would make it easier to cancel it in the future and threaten to turn it from a required event to a discretionary one.

Eliasson devoted considerable time attending seminars and conferences hosted by DC's think tank community. It was an excellent place to meet high-level experts on neutral ground, expand his contacts, and get a sense of what new ideas were brewing in Washington, which Eliasson regarded as modern-day Rome.

He was often asked to participate in special projects. In his final year in Washington, he was part of a simulated exercise broadcast by the BBC in the United Kingdom and ABC News in the United States in which former heads of state and national security officials played government officials responding to a bioterrorist attack. Eliasson was designated the Swedish prime minister in the table exercise and used the forum to urge a focus on a global, rather than a national, response. "We live in a time of new threats. And we need new responses. This shows we are not prepared. We don't have the right organizational structures for these responses, so we must be careful how we move ahead," he said during the mock deliberations.[4]

Eliasson's most enduring accomplishment during his ambassadorship was winning approval in Stockholm and Washington to build a new embassy, the House of Sweden, on the shores of the Potomac near the John F. Kennedy Center for the Performing Arts. After years of discussion, Eliasson helped close the deal, which he described as a consequential decision to reposition and repackage Sweden in Washington. "This is the most powerful country in the history of the world, and we need a showpiece for Sweden," he said in 2002, when announcing approval of the new embassy. Construction began in 2004 and the new embassy opened in the fall of 2006.

Sweden's ambassadors typically serve in Washington for five years, but this is not a hard and fast rule. As he neared that point, Eliasson pondered his options. Kerstin had returned to Sweden a year earlier to become deputy minister of higher education and research. He was eager to join her but was also intrigued at the prospect of staying in Washington for an additional year.

Then an unexpected opportunity arose. The possibility to become president of the UN General Assembly. "That changed everything," he said.

Eliasson's tenure as Sweden's ambassador to the United States was very successful. He served during two very close American presidential elections of 2000 and 2004, the terrorist attack of September 11, 2001, and the wars in Afghanistan and Iraq that were triggered, or justified, by the attacks. He significantly raised Sweden's profile in the United States and was invited into high-level policy discussions.

He was proud of his service and enjoyed almost every minute of it. But he was delighted to return to the United Nations and New York in the summer of 2005.

CHAPTER 3

Addicted to the United Nations

INSTANT ATTRACTION

Jan Eliasson once made a confession at a conference in Washington, DC, that would have surprised no one who knows him. "I'm addicted to the UN," he said. "It's in my veins." This addiction lasted for most of Eliasson's professional career and has taken several forms: a passion to understand, explain, and reform the global body along with a desire to make the UN work more effectively and live up to the lofty ideals it is based on.

He had frequent contact and collaboration with the United Nations throughout his career. First, as an aide to Swedish statesman Olof Palme, Eliasson became a rising Swedish diplomat; eventually he would become Sweden's ambassador to the UN, the UN's first under-secretary-general for humanitarian affairs, participant on several UN-related advisory boards, special envoy to Darfur, president of the UN General Assembly, and finally deputy secretary-general.

Serving in and around the UN for four decades, Eliasson has worked with every secretary-general since Kurt Waldheim in 1980 and hundreds of diplomats, staffers, and political leaders. He knows the UN's hallways, conference rooms, mores, moods, traditions, rules, and procedures—both formal and informal.

Eliasson's attraction to the United Nations is palpable and easy to understand. The UN is honored in Sweden as a principled and vital global organization in which it has earned a respected voice. The UN's professed values align closely with Sweden's. It was here that Dag Hammarskjöld, a Swedish civil servant, became the second secretary-general in 1953 and served with distinction, making his nation proud. The UN is the ultimate stage for multilateral diplomacy. This is the venue in which Eliasson operated effectively for four decades and served in a wider range of capacities than anyone in its history.

REVERENCE FOR THE UNITED NATIONS

Eliasson strongly supports the underlying premise of the UN—that nations of the world send their most skilled representatives to gather, discuss, and decide issues of global concern. He enthusiastically endorses the professed values of the UN. Somewhat theatrically, he carries a copy of the UN Charter in his pocket and quotes from it liberally, especially its opening words: "We the Peoples of the United Nations determined to save succeeding generations from the scourge of war." In his view, this means that the UN's founders were intensely—and primarily—focused on the well-being of individual people rather than nations or regional groups. He supports the four central aims of the UN: to safeguard peace and security, to reaffirm faith in fundamental human rights, to uphold respect for international law, and to promote social progress and better living standards.[1]

Eliasson sees the UN Charter as a wise, even profound, document that expresses essential values and creates viable institutions. He frequently refers to chapter 6, the Pacific Settlement of Disputes, and especially Article 33. He relishes the word "pacific," as in peaceful, and can cite this sentence by memory: "The parties to any dispute, the continuance of which is likely to endanger the maintenance of international peace and security, shall, first of all, seek a solution by negotiation, enquiry, mediation, conciliation, arbitration, judicial settlement, resort to regional agencies or arrangements, or other peaceful means of their own choice." He refers to these explicit references to diplomacy as "Christmas Eve for diplomats." Eliasson built his career on these instruments and techniques, especially negotiation and mediation.

Eliasson considers the UN to be the main stage of global diplomacy. He understands its history, cites resolutions from decades ago, and personally knew six of the nine secretaries-general. He has spent innumerable hours in the meeting rooms of the Security Council and the General Assembly, which he describes as a "Cathedral of Peace." He is delighted that the UN's main headquarters is in New York City, a city he sees as the embodiment of an open, energetic, and tolerant multicultural world.

He believes important questions of war and peace are appropriately discussed in this institution. While he has enormous respect for the UN's work in the field and repeatedly says this is where it is at its best, the truth is that he loves the energy and challenge of UN diplomacy in New York City. If some lament the tedium of UN debates, Eliasson relishes the vibrancy and complexity of diplomacy in the global body.

Eliasson is convinced the UN makes a difference in the lives of people and societies. He acknowledges that while it is deeply flawed, the UN does much that is productive and life-enhancing: feeding hundreds of millions of people, vaccinating about half the world's children, negotiating to save the ozone layer, assembling hundreds of treaties that make daily life safer, curbing the spread of nuclear weapons, deploying dozens of peacekeeping missions around the world, helping end colonization, assisting more than tens of millions of refugees and displaced people, curtailing Ebola, and advocating for rights for the disadvantaged. At various times at the UN, he distributed wallet-size cards that summarized the organization's tangible accomplishments.

Eliasson frequently describes himself as "a friend, but not an uncritical friend, of the UN." He believes that if the UN were eliminated it would have to be created again—and the result would likely be far less successful than it was the first time.

Eliasson is strongly attracted to the craft and mission of multilateral diplomacy—the work that occurs in institutions and at conferences when three or more countries gather to consider issues and problems.

Multilateral diplomacy is his milieu. He is outgoing, enjoys people, remembers names, is a generalist who can master details, speaks multiple languages, including impeccable English, and has a deep interest in, and memory about, global issues. He is a natural leader; he is aggressive but not overbearing, relentless but also patient, persuasive, tactful, and discreet. Eliasson has the skills, personality, and cast of mind of a successful multilateral diplomat. He is a shrewd negotiator, excellent at building personal relationships, and adept at taking charge. He can read a room, pick up nuances, whip votes, hone language, forge compromises, and synthesize ideas. He is a skilled wordsmith, has considerable stamina, is able to keep track of multiple issues, understands important rules and procedures, and masters seemingly technical issues that often have broad political implications.

Like many participants in multilateral diplomacy, Eliasson can get caught up in what has been called its "heady atmosphere," in which there is often great drama with little substance. The challenge of bringing a negotiation to a successful conclusion can sometimes become an end unto itself.

UN ROLE MODELS

As Eliasson's career unfolded he embraced role models who shaped his aspirations and nurtured his development. Not surprisingly for a Swede with a deep reverence for the UN, Eliasson's diplomatic ideal was Dag Hammarskjöld, the UN's second secretary-general and its best. He was a stellar Swedish civil servant who, when given the opportunity, showed world-class diplomatic skills and operated masterfully in international affairs.

The son of Sweden's prime minister during World War I, Hammarskjöld was an economist who steadily ascended the ranks of Sweden's civil service, becoming deputy finance minister, chair of the Bank of Sweden, and deputy foreign minister. He was a compromise—and a surprise—choice to become the UN secretary-general in 1953, following the resignation of Trygve Lie of Norway. Hammarskjöld was courageous, innovative, and a major actor in global affairs throughout the 1950s up to his death in a mysterious 1961 plane crash.

Hammarskjöld's record and legacy encouraged Eliasson to enter diplomacy. He was impressed by Hammarskjöld's values and diplomatic skills, the range of his UN accomplishments, and his ability to integrate art and culture into his life and work.

Several of Eliasson's diplomatic mentors worked for Hammarskjöld in their youth and regaled him with stories about the great man. Eliasson frequently quoted Hammarskjöld, particularly in the context of combining vision and practicality. "Never look down to test the ground before taking your next step: only he who keeps his eye fixed on the far horizon will find his right road." He also quoted Hammarskjöld in the context of resiliency. "When the morning's freshness has been replaced by the weariness of the midday, when the leg muscles give under the strain, the climb seems endless, and suddenly nothing will go quite as you wish—it is then that you must not hesitate."

In 2011 Eliasson delivered the prestigious Dag Hammarskjöld lecture at the University of Uppsala. The occasion, the fiftieth anniversary of Hammarskjöld's death, was especially meaningful and Eliasson worked on his remarks for a full month. Eliasson lavished praise on Hammarskjöld. "There are many reasons for the glow of his memory: his integrity, courage and impartiality; his diplomatic skills and attachment to the UN Charter; his championing of the rights of smaller and weaker nations," Eliasson told the packed audience. "Personally, I am impressed by his cool composure in crisis situations. And I am fascinated and intrigued by his passionate involvement in art, music, literature, philosophy, religion, as well as his love of nature, in parallel with the demanding tasks that confronted him as UN secretary-general." Eliasson said Hammarskjöld established for himself, and the UN, a diplomatic and moral platform during the fraught years of the Cold War. Hammarskjöld's ability to see the connection between issues and to advance peace and security, human rights, and development seamlessly was a model for the future.[2]

Eliasson later learned that Secretary-General Ban Ki-moon studied his tribute to Hammarskjöld when he was considering Eliasson to serve as deputy secretary-general. Ban presumably liked what he read.

One of Eliasson's final projects as a UN official was to support an intense examination of the circumstances of Hammarskjöld's death. Eliasson believes, based on expert testimony, that there was a distinct possibility that Hammarskjöld had been assassinated rather than killed accidentally in the plane crash. Several UN probes seem to confirm Eliasson's belief.

If Hammarskjöld was Eliasson's exalted diplomatic ideal, Brian Urquhart was the diplomat he most admired up close and frequently described as a mentor. Although Urquhart was a generation older than Eliasson, the two men knew each other well and worked together on various projects. Eliasson developed deep respect, almost veneration, for Urquhart, who had served as a British intelligence officer in World War II and was one of the first Allied soldiers to witness German concentration camps. Urquhart joined the UN at its launch in 1945. He served over the next four decades as a key aide to five secretaries-general and directed political affairs and peacekeeping operations around the world. He was the under-secretary-general for political affairs from 1972 to 1986. One profile described him as resourceful, irreverent, and unflappable, saying that "Mr. Urquhart blended qualities of a globetrotting adventurer and a determined international civil servant."[3]

Urquhart's career married longevity and consequence, idealism and practicality. He was also a UN historian who wrote important biographies of Hammarskjöld and Ralph Bunche, a skilled diplomatic contemporary. Urquhart's own memoir, *A Life in Peace and War*, is often described as one of the best books ever written about the UN's history, purposes, and principles.

Eliasson respected Urquhart's commitment to the UN, his pragmatism, and his effectiveness. The *Washington Post*'s obituary of Urquhart included a photo of him presenting Eliasson with the Dag Hammarskjöld Award. Urquhart was Eliasson's direct link to the UN's founding generation.

Andrew Gilmour, a former UN official and Urquhart aide, says he was "imbued with integrity, ethical standards, courage, and compassion. But at the same time, he had the acutest understanding of the harsh realities, practical constraints, and murky politicking that prevent international ideals from being put into practice. An idealist, but far from starry-eyed. A moralist but the least self-righteous one imaginable. One of the world's leading diplomats, but direct, sincere, irreverent, and unpretentious. His points were delivered in a manner that was often humorous, self-deprecating, and disarmingly modest. The result was that almost every interlocutor felt at ease and able to trust him."[4]

This is also an apt description of Eliasson.

UN ANTAGONISTS

Eliasson got along with most people during his diplomatic career. He had mentors, mentees, peers, and rivals, but few enemies. It may not be completely correct to describe John Bolton, the US ambassador to the UN, as an enemy, but he and Eliasson were antagonists who clashed repeatedly during Eliasson's General Assembly presidency in 2005 and 2006.

While they were both from working-class backgrounds, Eliasson and Bolton were different in almost every other conceivable way. Eliasson was a dapper, multilingual, polished, exuberant, extroverted, career diplomat. He loved diplomacy and believed passionately in the United Nations. He understood, and was skillful at, multilateral diplomacy and respected the norms and processes of the UN.

John Bolton was a brusque, combative, and unapologetic American nationalist who spoke of the UN with a mixture of ridicule and scorn. "There is no United Nations," he once said. "There is an international community that occasionally can be led by the only real power left in the world, and that's the United States, when it suits our interests and when we can get others to go along." On another occasion, Bolton was even more withering. "The Secretariat Building in New York has 38 stories. If you lost ten stories today, it wouldn't make a bit of difference." According to *The Economist* magazine, Bolton was "the most controversial ambassador ever sent by America to the United Nations," and his most striking trait during his time in New York was "his inability, or his unwillingness, to make friends and build alliances in an organization where networking, compromise, and consensus are the order of the day."[5]

Almost immediately upon Bolton's arrival at the UN he battled with Eliasson and others, over a draft summary of the coming summit of global leaders. Eliasson described the document's proposals as groundbreaking and consequential while Bolton dismissed them as verbose and vacuous.

In Bolton's memoir about his time at the UN, *Surrender Is Not an Option: Defending America at the United Nations,* he took frequent shots at Eliasson. In one passage he wrote that Eliasson was in "full, dreamy Dag Hammarskjöld mode." In another, he dismissed him as "yet another foreigner who 'understood' us better than we did our selves." He hammered

Eliasson's "leftist tilt and excessive view of his own importance" and derided him as "President of the World Eliasson."[6]

Eliasson is restrained in his assessment of Bolton, but his skepticism about the man and his values is apparent and palpable. He chuckles that Bolton's comparisons of him to Hammarskjöld are a "badge of honor" for any Swedish diplomat. He also recalls meeting Bolton's wife at a UN reception and having a pleasant conversation with her. Bolton later told Eliasson that his wife was quite impressed with the Swedish diplomat. "The subtext being, he couldn't understand why," Eliasson says with a smile.

If Bolton was an opponent from central casting for a liberal internationalist such as Eliasson, his battles with Miguel de Serpa Soares were more subtle. Serpa Soares has been the under-secretary-general for legal affairs and chief legal counsel for more than a decade. Prior to his work at the UN, he had been a legal expert in Portugal's foreign ministry with extensive international legal experience.

During Eliasson's tenure as the deputy secretary-general, he came into sharp conflict with Serpa Soares over several human rights issues. Eliasson urged the world body to acknowledge past mistakes, apologize to victims, and make generous restitution in several specific cases. He was deeply troubled by the UN's accidental culpability in bringing cholera to Haiti in 2010 when UN peacekeepers from Nepal inadvertently infected Haitian citizens. The outbreak killed more than 9,000 and made hundreds of thousands seriously ill. Eliasson pressed for a strong and clear UN apology and generous financial compensation for the families of the victims. Serpa Soares and his UN legal team feared an apology might carry legal significance that the organization should avoid and could complicate its immunity status. Serpa Soares proposed voluntary payments to victims combined with an official statement of regret.

Serpa Soares also opposed a major initiative that Eliasson developed to significantly elevate the UN's commitment to human rights through its Human Rights Up Front program. Serpa Soares resisted it during Eliasson's tenure as deputy secretary-general and helped scuttle it altogether after Eliasson left the UN at the end of 2016. Aides said Eliasson and Serpa Soares had a thinly disguised antipathy for each other, rooted in different personalities, temperaments, and responsibilities. For Eliasson, Serpa Soares's defensive attitude and approach imperiled the UN's most fundamental values.

UN Diplomat

Eliasson followed UN issues during the early phase of his diplomatic career but did not have intense involvement with the global body until 1980.

The Iran-Iraq war broke out in September of that year and several months later Olof Palme, then Sweden's opposition leader, was asked by UN Secretary-General Kurt Waldheim to try to bring an end to the conflict. Palme and Sweden's foreign minister agreed that Eliasson should serve as Palme's chief aide. Hence the unexpected phone call that led Eliasson and Palme to fly to New York for meetings at the UN, and then onto the region, shuttling between Iran and Iraq.

Eliasson spent much of the 1980s working as part of a UN team to end the Iran-Iraq war. This was a turning point in his career. He worked closely with Palme and observed his hard-charging approach and his shrewd political and diplomatic skills. For five years they conferred on long plane trips and in hotel rooms preparing for their negotiations. Palme was relentless and strategic. Eliasson was struck by Palme's "almost insatiable interest in foreign policy."

While part of their work was conducted in the region, Eliasson was frequently at UN headquarters in New York. He worked with senior officials, including Waldheim and Urquhart, as well as others from the UN Secretariat and Security Council, including top diplomats from the Permanent Five—the United States, the United Kingdom, France, China, and Russia.

Eliasson collaborated closely with Palme on the Iran-Iraq war from 1980 until Palme's death in 1986. Following Palme's assassination, Secretary-General Javier Pérez de Cuéllar took over the UN mediation effort and later named Eliasson as his personal representative for Iran and Iraq. In 1988 the UN Security Council passed Resolution 598 that helped end the war. Eliasson grimly observed that the final package the two war-weary nations accepted was similar to the one that Palme and his team suggested in the early 1980s. In the interim, the war claimed an estimated two million dead and wounded, and two societies and an entire region were deeply traumatized.

Later that year Eliasson was selected by his government to serve as Sweden's ambassador to the UN, a highly coveted post in Swedish diplomacy. His predecessor, Anders Ferm, was another Palme protégé who did not want to leave and felt that he was being forced out. He eventually relented, but the transition was awkward and tense.

Eliasson served at the UN as the Cold War wound down and relished the idea that the world body appeared poised to play the large and constructive role that its founders envisioned. He attended Mikhail Gorbachev's historic UN address on December 7, 1988, and had a moment to compliment the Soviet Union leader on his visionary speech.

While serving as Sweden's ambassador to the UN, Eliasson was also elected in 1991 as a vice president of the UN Economic and Social Council. He helped draft a resolution establishing the UN's responsibilities in the humanitarian realm. He participated in several weeks of intense talks in Geneva developing this resolution. At one point he left the negotiations to visit his seriously ailing father in Sweden. Eliasson reluctantly acceded to his father's request that he return to work in Geneva. Sadly, in the midst of the negotiations, his father passed away.

On December 18, 1991, the UN General Assembly approved Resolution 46/182, which Eliasson and others call the UN's Humanitarian Magna Carta. It established the UN Department of Humanitarian Affairs and created the position of Under-Secretary-General for Humanitarian Affairs and Emergency Relief Coordinator.[7] In February 1992, Eliasson was asked by Secretary-General Boutros Boutros-Ghali to become the first to hold the new position.

Though he was intrigued by the challenge to work at a new position that dealt with matters he cared deeply about, Eliasson was reluctant to step down as Sweden's UN ambassador. But he chose to accept and served in the post from 1992 to 1994. It was ultimately a difficult time for him. He tried to build a new organization, address crises exploding around the world, and deal with the secretary-general, who was aloof and abrasive and not convinced the UN should be deeply involved in humanitarian matters.

Eliasson traveled extensively to oversee the UN's humanitarian response to crises in Somalia, Sudan, Mozambique, Liberia, Angola, South Africa, and the Balkans. His work in Somalia was especially depressing, as he sought to navigate through anarchy on the ground while seeing young children die before his eyes. "I felt like the fireman who was working the day shift and night shift and always arrived to find burned down houses. It was a disgrace for the international community to be passive witnesses to the Somalia tragedy for so long. We simply came too late."

Secretary-General Boutros-Ghali restricted Eliasson's travel as well as his staff's. At one point he accused Eliasson of being obsessed with humanitarian issues. "I thought that was my job, Mr. Secretary-General," Eliasson replied. He was frustrated that his position was largely reactive, rushing from one disaster to the next without dealing with underlying causes. He likened his work to putting band-aids on infected wounds or relying on an umbrella during a hurricane.

Eliasson left the UN in 1994 and returned to Sweden, first taking a sabbatical at Uppsala to study and teach about conflict prevention. He became Sweden's deputy foreign minister later that year. He continued to follow the UN, but at a distance. As mentioned earlier, he served as Sweden's successful ambassador to the United States from 2000 until 2005. The Swedish government decided to seek the presidency of the UN General Assembly for the 2005–2006 session. After an effective lobbying campaign by the Swedes, Eliasson was selected for the position in November 2004, although his formal election did not take place until June of 2005.

PRESIDENT OF THE GENERAL ASSEMBLY

In terms of diplomatic protocol, the president of the UN General Assembly is the highest-ranking UN official. However, the presidency is a one-year position that rotates between five regional groups and has a heavy ceremonial aspect. The president, or PGA, presides over the General Assembly, which, in 2005, comprised 191 ambassadors from the UN's member states. He or she is charged with setting the agenda, overseeing debates, and representing the General Assembly at political and diplomatic functions. The General Assembly is one of the principal entities created by the UN Charter. The others are the Security Council, Economic and Social Council, Trusteeship Council, International Court of Justice, and Secretariat.

The General Assembly is the UN's most representative body. It holds a general debate in New York each year from September to December and convenes special sessions at other times to address pressing issues. Its key functions are to debate and make recommendations related to international peace and security. It elects nonpermanent members to the fifteen-member Security Council and other UN bodies. The General Assembly also appoints the secretary-general based on the Security Council's recommendation. Its most concrete responsibility is to approve the UN budget. Each member of the General Assembly has a vote.

Eliasson was officially elected president of the sixtieth General Assembly in June 2005, though his term didn't begin until September of that year. UN tradition holds that the incoming PGA serve as a kind of co-president with their predecessor. So from June until September Eliasson served alongside Jean Ping of Gabon, the president of the fifty-ninth General Assembly.

Upon his election in June, Eliasson addressed the General Assembly. He observed that his election had special significance for his country since 2005 was the one hundredth anniversary of Dag Hammarskjöld's birth. Eliasson praised Secretary-General Kofi Annan's pending reform proposal as the most comprehensive and cohesive plan to strengthen the UN since its creation in 1945. Eliasson said the UN and the global community were facing "a test of multilateralism" as they confronted the triple challenges of development, security, and human rights. "The three are intertwined and affect and reinforce each other." He said the UN's central objectives were to end suffering and improve lives. "The litmus test and measuring rod for UN reforms must be the difference they make for the people and crisis areas around the world: for the starving child, the AIDS stricken mother, the war-torn country, the polluted river, the desperate refugee. What I call the 'field tests' should be applied to all reform proposals."

His presidency, he pledged, would be guided by the values and principles that are the pillars of Sweden's foreign policy: belief in multilateral cooperation, the imperative of prevention, respect for the rule of law and human rights, solidarity with the poor, concern for the rights of women and the safety of children, and protection of the environment. "This is the essence of the reform project of the UN: building a UN which effectively and legitimately responds to the urgent needs around the world and adds value to our work for security, prosperity, and a life in dignity for all. Making real progress to reach this end would be our most important contribution to the historic test of multilateralism which we are now facing."[8]

Throughout the summer Eliasson and Ping worked with Annan and his team on the ambitious reform proposal that would be considered at the World Summit meeting of global leaders in September. The proposal outlined the agenda of the United Nations for the upcoming year. It mandated that Eliasson undertake several major initiatives during his presidency, including creating a Peacebuilding Commission and a Human Rights Council.

Meanwhile, Bolton, the US Ambassador to the UN, arrived in New York that August and immediately began trying to unravel the reform proposal. He argued that the lengthy document should be stripped down to a bare-bones summary of just two or three pages. Eliasson believed the proposal was "groundbreaking and historic" while Bolton derided it as empty rhetoric. Among other things, the document endorsed the Responsibility to Protect doctrine, which called for a global norm declaring that the international community might deploy forces, if necessary and approved by the Security Council, in countries to prevent genocide, war crimes, and crimes against humanity.[9]

Following the approval of the proposal, Eliasson and his staff developed a timetable to address the major issues sequentially. First, create the Peacebuilding Commission, then establish a Human Rights Council, and finally, attempt management reform and craft an antiterrorism strategy. Eliasson is a firm proponent of sequential diplomacy, dealing with one major issue at a time, rather than linkage diplomacy, which combines negotiations on various issues.

Over the course of his year as president of the UN General Assembly, Eliasson succeeded at most of his goals; the Peacebuilding Commission was approved in December 2005 and the Human Rights Council in March 2006. An antiterrorism strategy was concluded in the late summer of 2006; however, management reform languished. His presidency of the UN General Assembly was considered impressive and successful by most UN observers.

In a statement at the end of his term in September 2006, Eliasson was celebratory in a subdued way. "You have, in my view, revitalized the General Assembly by your willingness and ability to take strong and decisive action. But our work is not finished. Many items on our reform agenda represent work in progress." He praised the diplomats in the General Assembly for rising "from the national to the international" on many occasions. "This year's reforms were unprecedented—but not enough," adding that the UN still needed to firmly establish that international cooperation is the best way to manage global affairs. "Do not hesitate as you carry the torch of multilateralism forward in this troubled and uncertain world," he declared.[10]

DEPUTY SECRETARY-GENERAL

In the final months as president of the General Assembly, Eliasson was named Sweden's foreign minister by Prime Minister Göran Persson. This was a surprise promotion and a singular honor for Eliasson. He was the first career diplomat since World War II to serve in the position. However, the timing was less than perfect for several reasons. Eliasson was consumed with his UN responsibilities and the Persson government was facing an election that October. If the government was defeated, Eliasson's tenure as foreign minister would last only six months—which is exactly what happened. Eliasson later mused, "I would have loved to have had four years as foreign minister. There is so much I would have liked to have done. But it was not to be."

After his General Assembly presidency ended in September and his tenure as Sweden's foreign minister concluded in October 2006, Eliasson took a few months off. Ban Ki-moon, the incoming secretary-general, inquired whether Eliasson wished to be considered for the position of his deputy. Eliasson had just completed five years as Sweden's ambassador in the United States followed by a busy and consequential year as president of the UN General Assembly and Sweden's foreign minister. It simply wasn't the right time to remain at the UN in New York.

However, several weeks later Eliasson accepted a UN assignment, based in Stockholm, to mediate the war in Darfur in 2007 and 2008, which will be discussed later. When that assignment ended, Eliasson returned to Sweden and worked on numerous projects from 2008 to 2012, including establishing WaterAid, an international water advocacy group, and serving on the UN's Millennium Development Goals Advocacy Panel. The MDGs aspired to sharply curtail poverty in the world.

In early 2012 Ban again reached out to Eliasson and asked if he would now consider becoming the deputy secretary-general. The two diplomats had known each other since 2000 when they were both deputy foreign ministers. Before making the offer, Ban had read Eliasson's 2011 Dag Hammarskjöld lecture in which Eliasson made a vigorous case for the relevance of the UN and emphasized the importance of connecting security, development, and human rights. Eliasson was interested in the post and asked for a few days to discuss it with his wife. When Ban called back, Eliasson accepted with the understanding that he would play a senior role and have a broad portfolio that included peace and security, development, and human rights. He would attend key meetings, work on special projects, and represent Ban and the UN around the world. He would not be the chief operating officer of the UN Secretariat but would function more as an American-style vice president who had both substantive and representational responsibilities.[11]

Eliasson served as the UN deputy secretary-general from July 2012 to December 2016, when Ban's term ended. This was a dream job for Eliasson, especially given that he was in his early seventies when he began—well past retirement age for many diplomats. It allowed him to return to the UN, an institution he revered, to become its second in command, and to serve as the second-highest ranking Swede in UN history.

Eliasson enjoyed the high-profile job with a wide-ranging portfolio that put him in the middle of issues he cared about, including development, human rights, nonproliferation, public health, sustainability, and water. He traveled extensively, represented the UN around the world, and worked on crises in Syria, Haiti, Sri Lanka, Iran, Yemen, and Ukraine. There were days he was briefed on three major crises. The consummate diplomat, Eliasson was careful not to overshadow Ban. He was respectful, deferential, and deflected the suggestion that he had his own agenda by brandishing his worn copy of the UN Charter stating that *it* was his only agenda. As deputy secretary-general, he had many jobs and one overarching mission: to describe and defend the UN ideal and to make the institution become a better functioning leader of the multilateral system.

In the pages that follow we will examine specific diplomatic episodes from Eliasson's UN career: his advocacy for human rights; his efforts to mediate the war in Darfur; his endeavor to develop, promote, and implement the Sustainable Development Goals; and his long-standing effort to foster a culture of prevention in the world.

PART III
EPISODES IN DIPLOMACY

CHAPTER 4

Negotiating for Human Rights

THE GENEVA CHALLENGE

Jan Eliasson, then president of the UN General Assembly, traveled to Geneva in June 2006 to both celebrate and challenge. He had spent much of the past year in tense, complex, high-stakes negotiations to win approval by the General Assembly of a Human Rights Council for the United Nations.

Deploying his best diplomatic skills, Eliasson channeled broad, but diffuse, support for the new council into a concrete proposal that withstood intense skepticism from the United States, followed by outright opposition. It was multilateral diplomacy at its most challenging and the inaugural meeting of this council was, Eliasson believed, a cause for celebration. However, he knew the hard work had just begun. He played a central role in creating a new institution and now faced the even more difficult task of making it work—and making it worth his efforts and those of the UN.

Secretary-General Kofi Annan joined Eliasson for the inaugural meeting of the Human Rights Council. Annan had proposed the concept of a new body several years earlier and had been an effective advocate for it. Speaking to the members of the council, Annan said it needed to represent a "clean break from the past." The Human Rights Council was replacing the UN's once successful, but now largely discredited, Commission on Human Rights.

51

"What must be apparent, above all, is a change of culture," Annan declared. "Never allow this council to become caught up in political point scoring or petty maneuver. Think always of those whose rights are denied—whether those rights are civil and political or economic, social, and cultural; whether those people are perishing from brutal treatment by arbitrary rules, or from ignorance, hunger, and disease."[1]

Eliasson then took to the podium. He basked, briefly, in his hard-fought success, calling this opening session historic and describing it as "a new chapter in the United Nations' work on human rights." He then leveled a challenge to the delegates. "Now you have to show determination and courage to translate intentions and words to the changing of realities and taking action. This requires from us all statesmanship and preparedness not only to examine each other but also to examine ourselves."

Eliasson argued that by creating the council the UN now had a "sharper instrument to promote and protect human rights" but this new tool still needed to be used effectively. He summarized the protracted and contentious diplomacy that led to the successful vote the previous month to create the council. The new council, he believed, represented renewed respect for human dignity and hope. The first year would be crucial to establish its credibility and to demonstrate its commitment to "place the human being in the center," Eliasson said.[2]

Reflecting later on that moment and the intense diplomacy that had preceded it, Eliasson said it was the most difficult and important project of his General Assembly presidency. "It was a hell of a negotiation," he said. "I planned it carefully."

THE UN AND HUMAN RIGHTS

The United Nations was created in 1945 in response to the stunningly egregious violations of human rights in the previous decades. Not surprisingly, the UN Charter has many references to human rights. The preamble begins with these words: "We the Peoples of the United Nations determined to save succeeding generations from the scourge of war, which twice in our lifetime has brought untold sorrow to mankind, and to reaffirm faith in the fundamental human rights, in the dignity and worth of the human person, in the equal rights of men and women and of nations large and small."[3]

The UN Charter's first chapter describes the new body's purposes and principles, which include "promoting and encouraging respect for human rights and for fundamental freedoms for all without distinction as to race, sex, language, or religion." The nascent UN created the Commission on Human Rights. It first met in 1947 and was chaired by Eleanor Roosevelt, the former first lady of the United States, and a relentless champion for human rights. Drafting the Universal Declaration of Human Rights was one of the commission's first acts. Adopted by the UN on December 10, 1948, it outlines thirty rights and freedoms that all should enjoy, and it remains the basis for international human rights law to this day. It is regarded as the bedrock of international human rights law and has inspired dozens of legally binding human rights treaties in countries around the world.

The Universal Declaration's first article begins by saying that "All human beings are born free and equal in dignity and rights." The declaration was later supplemented by the International Covenant on Civil and Political Rights and the International Covenant on Economic, Social, and Cultural Rights. These three documents—the declaration and the two covenants—are seen as the International Bill of Rights.[4]

With fundamental human rights identified, the Commission on Human Rights worked for decades to monitor, and publicly report on, respect for human rights in specific countries. Initially it focused on promoting human rights and helping states develop treaties. It later investigated and condemned violators.

However, the commission was hampered by the frequent presence of member countries who were, themselves, egregious violators of human rights. Their motive for joining the panel appeared to primarily be self-protection from scrutiny and criticism. By the 1990s the Commission on Human Rights had become the target of ridicule, criticism, and frustration. In 1993, in an attempt to regain respect and trust, the UN created the post of High Commissioner for Human Rights. The commission itself remained but was more of an embarrassment and a hindrance to promoting human rights than an advocate for the cause.

The Secretary-General Proposes

A decade later, Secretary-General Kofi Annan decided to advance a broad reform agenda with an eye toward the UN's sixtieth anniversary in 2005. He established a high-level panel to review the UN's work and propose needed reforms. The result was a 2004 report called "A More Secure World: Our Shared Responsibility." The report outlined areas that required rethinking and reform. It scorched the Commission on Human Rights, saying that its work had been "undermined by eroding credibility and professionalism. States have sought membership on the commission not to strengthen human rights but to protect themselves against criticism or to criticize others." The panel said member states should consider replacing the commission with a Human Rights Council that would have a sharper mission and more institutional strength within the UN system.[5]

The following year Annan issued a wide-ranging reform plan called "In Larger Freedom," which proposed major changes to the UN's practices and institutions. The report argued that championing human rights remained an essential mission of the UN, but reforms were essential for the body to be effective. Annan proposed strengthening the office of the High Commissioner for Human Rights and replacing the Commission on Human Rights with a smaller, more selective and nimble Human Rights Council whose members would be elected by two-thirds majorities in the General Assembly. "The creation of the council would accord human rights a more authoritative position, corresponding to the primacy of human rights in the Charter of the United Nations," he said, adding that those elected to the council should embody the highest human rights standards. Annan argued the UN needed a leaner, more credible, more empowered human rights body. "We have reached a point at which the commission's declining credibility has cast a shadow on the reputation of the United Nations system as a whole, and where piecemeal reforms will not be enough." The gap between what the UN promised on human rights and what it delivered had widened. "The answer is not to draw back from an ambitious human rights agenda, but to make the improvements that will enable our machinery to live up to the world's expectations."[6]

Annan presented his reform proposal to global leaders at the World Summit held at the UN in September 2005. The final document approved by world leaders called for a new Human Rights Council. "The council will be responsible for promoting universal respect for the protection of all human rights and fundamental freedoms for all, without distinction of any kind and in a fair and equal manner. . . . It should also promote effective coordination and the mainstreaming of human rights within the UN system."[7] The president of the UN General Assembly, Jan Eliasson, was charged to create this council.

ELIASSON TAKES OVER

After assuming the presidency of the General Assembly in September 2005, Eliasson first helped establish a Peacebuilding Commission to assist nations to rebuild after emerging from conflict. This was approved in December 2005. He then turned to the central challenge of his presidency—creating the new Human Rights Council. He brought to this project substantial experience both in the workings of the UN and in the realm of human rights. He knew the issues, the institutions, the players, the controversies, and the history.

In early October, Eliasson selected two cochairs to begin the preliminary work of soliciting the views of the then 191 members of the General Assembly. He chose Ricardo Alberto Arias of Panama and Dumisani Kumalo of South Africa to begin consultations with national delegations. They met with dozens of diplomats to discuss the proposed Human Rights Council, focusing on its status within the UN system, its mandate, functions, and the size and composition of its membership.

As discussions in the UN diplomatic community began, nongovernmental human rights advocacy groups weighed in. In a letter to Eliasson, Amnesty International, Freedom House, the World Federalist Movement, Refugees International, and other groups outlined their expectations for the new Human Rights Council. "The Human Rights Council must significantly enhance the UN's existing capacity to protect and promote human rights," they wrote. They argued that it should be elevated to a principal organ of the UN within five years, address matters related to the protection and promotion of human rights in any country, comprise states who are committed to human rights, and include members who were directly elected by a two-thirds vote of the General Assembly. "We believe that by incorporating each of the above elements the Human Rights Council will be able to fulfill the promise that engendered this reform. Given the inter-relationship of many of these issues, failure to secure any of these key points would compromise the entire effort," the letter warned.[8]

Eliasson's plan was for Arias and Kumalo to assemble the ideas of UN diplomats and civil society and draft a proposal in consultation with his office. He had his staff closely monitor the progress of the discussions and formulate ideas that Eliasson could introduce in the event of a deadlock. The two cochairs worked assiduously from October 2005 until February 2006 and developed a framework. They then told Eliasson they had gone as far as they could, but a number of important issues were unresolved. "They put it on my lap," Eliasson said.

Stepping forward, Eliasson sent a letter to all the UN ambassadors. He noted that Arias and Kumalo had held more than thirty consultations with their fellow diplomats, had accomplished a great deal, and that their proposal would be refined by his office. "In order to move our work toward its conclusion I will conduct intense consultations over the coming days. I look forward to meeting any of you who wish to do so." It was now time to unite around a plan to create a Human Rights Council that would strengthen the United Nations human rights machinery.

Several weeks of intense discussions, detailed staff work, draft language, and tough negotiations ensued, much of which was conducted in Eliasson's presidential office. On February 23, Eliasson released a plan that he said was his best effort to formulate a draft resolution on the Human Rights Council that was workable and reflected the UN's aspirations. The new council would assume the role and responsibilities of the languishing Commission on Human Rights; make recommendations to the General Assembly on the further development of human rights law; promote the full implementation of human rights obligations undertaken by states; conduct universal periodic reviews of all UN member nations; promote the prevention of human rights violations; work in close cooperation with governments, regional organizations, national human rights organizations, and civil society; make recommendations on promoting and protecting human rights; and submit an annual report to the General Assembly.[9]

Under Eliasson's package, the Human Rights Council would consist of forty-seven members, down slightly from the commission's fifty-three. Countries would be elected by a simple majority of the General Assembly by secret ballot. The council would meet three times a year for no less than ten weeks annually. The General Assembly could, by a two-thirds vote, suspend members from the council who committed gross and systematic violations of human rights. Eliasson emphasized his proposal's inclusion of a universal periodic review provision. This was a new and important tool to ensure that the human rights records of all member nations were examined. It sought to make it clear that the council would be fair to all UN members.

Eliasson said the Human Rights Council would be a "truly new and different body—a fresh start." It would differ from the Commission on Human Rights in several crucial respects. It would be a subsidiary body of the General Assembly and as such would have a higher institutional standing than did the commission. It had a more effective way of convening sessions outside of its regular meeting time; members would serve two terms and then go off for a period. Council membership was open to all, and it would meet regularly throughout the year. Eliasson was clear that his draft was not just another step in the negotiating process. "This matter is now ripe for decision. We have traveled a long and arduous road to get to where we are today," Eliasson said, adding that the text was balanced and workable. Changing any provision could lead to renegotiating the entire plan—opening Pandora's box.

The human rights community considered Eliasson's draft a distinct improvement over the Commission on Human Rights but added that it did not go as far to protect human rights as many wished. "This is a historic opportunity that governments must not squander for selfish political interests," Amnesty International said in a statement. It added that the council was not as strong as it hoped. "While the president's text provides a sound basis on which to create a better body than the Commission on Human Rights, it must not be diluted further."[10] Eliasson's draft was immediately derided by John Bolton, the US ambassador to the UN. Bolton called Eliasson's proposal weak and said it did not assure that only committed supporters of human rights would sit on the council. He also accused Eliasson of drafting the plan behind closed doors with UN officials rather than conducting "real" negotiations between governments. "The strongest argument in favor of this draft," Bolton intoned, "is that it's not as bad as it could be."

Bolton wanted to reopen the discussions and develop a new package. Eliasson was skeptical of Bolton's goodwill, suspicious of his intentions, and doubtful that he had the multilateral diplomatic savvy to assemble a stronger alternative that could win approval. He had heard from other UN ambassadors that Bolton declined repeated opportunities to participate in drafting discussions and showed no interest in engaging on the proposed council. Eliasson told reporters that he had consulted widely over five months on the package and additional negotiations would not improve the text—but rather, would have everyone "going in circles." Eliasson made back-channel phone calls to US secretary of state Condoleezza Rice and Nicholas Burns, under secretary of state for political affairs, to explain his plan and determine if Bolton's views were those of the entire administration or just a conservative faction supported by Vice President Richard Cheney. He never got a clear answer.

Eliasson suffered a major blow several days later when the *New York Times* published a blistering critique of his plan. The op-ed was titled, "The Shame of the United Nations." It argued that UN leaders had "unwisely put their preference for multilateral consensus ahead of their duty to fight for the strongest possible human rights protections. A once promising reform proposal has been so watered down that it has become an ugly sham, offering cover to an unacceptable status quo. It should be renegotiated or rejected." The essay argued that members of the proposed council should be elected by two-thirds majorities, not simple majorities. It said that under Eliasson's plan members of the council would still be nominated by regional blocs without regard to their human rights performance. The op-ed dismissed the plan as a "pathetic draft" and praised Bolton, saying it hoped that "his refusal to go along with this shameful charade can produce something better."[11]

Eliasson was stunned and angered by the op-ed, which he believed was inaccurate, unfair, and harmful to the cause of human rights. "I thought it would sink our work," he said. He blamed himself for failing to adequately brief the press about his package. "I should have been much more attentive to the media." He worried that the mood among the champions of his plan sunk "so low" after the *New York Times* article.

However, other key leaders stepped forward to praise Eliasson's draft. Mary Robinson, the former president of Ireland, former UN High Commissioner for Human Rights, and a respected global leader, wrote an essay in the *International Herald Tribune* and the *New York Times* that lauded Eliasson's work. She said his plan was constructive and the best that could be agreed to at the time. "More talk will almost certainly produce a weaker council," she wrote. "While the new proposal is not all that human rights advocates hoped for, it is a clear improvement on the commission and has many positive aspects that can be welcomed."[12]

In another important development, several prominent Nobel Peace Prize laureates urged approval of Eliasson's plan. Writing a joint op-ed in the *New York Times*, Jimmy Carter, Óscar Arias, Kim Dae-jung, Shirin Ebadi, and Desmond Tutu argued that in "the global struggle for the advancement of human rights, the United Nations has reached a defining moment." Eliasson's draft was a significant and meaningful improvement over the existing commission and reopening negotiations would put at risk these gains and give those who preferred a weaker system another opportunity to do mischief. "Mr Eliasson has found a way forward that can bring everyone on board. Nearly 60 years after the adoption of the Universal Declaration of Human Rights, he has finally brought us to where we can begin to put principles over politics for the betterment of all."[13]

Eliasson decided to move ahead with the package in the General Assembly on March 15, 2006, and hoped to get unanimous consent, obviating the need for a formal vote. Most resolutions that are approved by the General Assembly are not put to a recorded vote but approved by unanimous consent. However, opponents of his plan signaled that they would seek a formal vote. "This was the hardest decision of my presidency. I broke the Holy Rule. Votes are very unusual in the General

Assembly. But it was necessary this time." He feared there might be a backlash in the US Congress, with possible cuts in American funds for UN programs.

In his statement to the General Assembly before the vote, Eliasson said the draft was the culmination of months of good faith negotiations. "We have reached a decisive moment, both for the promotion and protection of human rights and for effective multilateralism and the standing of the United Nations as a whole," he declared. He said his draft built on six decades of valuable work by the commission but also offered innovative and essential improvements. "This draft resolution represents a unique opportunity for a fresh start for human rights. The establishment of the Human Rights Council is a decision whose time has come. . . . No one part can now be added or subtracted in isolation without jeopardizing its balance, strength, and workability. This is a draft resolution whose sum is greater than its parts."[14] He called for the vote and UN General Assembly approved the resolution by a vote of 170 to 4. The United States, Israel, Marshall Islands, and Palau were the only countries that voted against it; Venezuela, Iran, and Belarus abstained.

Immediately after the vote, Bolton expressed disappointment. He said he appreciated Eliasson's goal to create an effective human rights body but "on too many issues the current text is not sufficiently improved." He said he remained concerned that human rights opponents could still get on the council and undermine the cause of human rights. "We had a historic opportunity to create a primary human rights organ in the UN poised to help those most in need and offer a hand to government to build what the Charter calls 'fundamental freedoms.'" The final package, he said, was a weak compromise.[15]

Eliasson was relieved by the vote but knew much work remained. About two months later, the General Assembly voted for the first slate of members to the Human Rights Council. Before that vote, Eliasson said that the General Assembly was about to begin "a new era in the United Nations' endeavors to promote and protect human rights. It is now time to implement this historic achievement." After the inaugural members of the council were elected, Eliasson said, "We are now witnessing a new beginning for the promotion and protection of human rights." The work would now shift to Geneva. The Human Rights Council must prove itself.

HUMAN RIGHTS COUNCIL

Jan Eliasson has remained keenly interested in human rights issues after leaving the UN presidency in 2006 and closely followed the work of the Human Rights Council. Sadly, the council has not met Eliasson's most profound hopes for a body that was a forceful, effective, and consistent human rights champion. Several unsavory governments who scorned civil rights were elected to the council. However, it did have significant accomplishments in monitoring human rights and investigating breaches. Eliasson and many human rights experts believe the creation of the regular review of the human rights records of all counties through the universal periodic review mechanism was a historic accomplishment. Other mechanisms have also proved important and constructive to examine human rights problems around the world. Commissions of inquiry, fact-finding missions, special sessions, and a complaint procedure have all been impactful.

The uneven and uncertain relationship of the United States with the Human Rights Council has limited its effectiveness. Presidents George W. Bush and Donald Trump kept the United States out of the council and consequently American influence in the body was minimal during their administrations. During the presidencies of Barack Obama and Joe Biden, the United States rejoined the council, made solid contributions, and significantly increased its effectiveness.

The council is the world's only intergovernmental body focused on human rights and thus shines an important spotlight on difficult issues. Like much else in multilateral diplomacy, especially at the UN, high-stakes negotiations often yield modest compromises rather than bold plans. This is true of the Human Rights Council and raises the hard question: was it worth all the time and diplomatic work? The Human Rights Council has been a consequential, if imperfect and flawed, body. It has done good in the world and Eliasson's contribution was crucial. He crafted and won approval of the best package that was possible at the time. And time was of the essence. The Human Rights Council has not revolutionized human rights throughout the world but has elevated and defended them. That is often the most that diplomacy can accomplish.

HUMAN RIGHTS UP FRONT

Six years later in 2012, when Eliasson returned to the UN as deputy secretary-general, he continued to argue that human rights should be regarded as one of the central pillars of the UN along with peace and security and development. Early in his tenure, Eliasson took on a high-profile human rights initiative. Several months after he returned to the UN, it received a disturbing internal report citing its failure to act during the final stages of Sri Lanka's 2009 bloody civil war. The review, by former UN official Charles Petrie, strongly criticized the UN's failure to effectively respond to a situation in which as many as 40,000 civilians were killed in the final phase of the war. Calling it a "grave failure," the Petrie report charged that UN officials in Sri Lanka failed to "stand up for the rights of the people they were mandated to assist." It said that "many senior UN staff simply did not perceive the prevention of killing of civilians as their responsibility."[16]

Secretary-General Ban Ki-moon was disturbed by the report and asked Eliasson to develop a response. Eliasson assembled a team, led by Andrew Gilmour, the political and human rights director in the secretary-general's office, to develop a plan to make the UN a more effective and consistent champion of human rights. The fundamental objective was to establish a commitment to protect human rights in the UN's organizational mindset and operations. Everyone working at the UN should believe that protecting human rights was an institutional responsibility.

Eliasson produced an internal document, the Human Rights Up Front action plan, which outlined a system-wide commitment by the UN to prevent human rights abuses and to respond aggressively and effectively when violations occurred. The overarching theme was that protecting human rights should be in the DNA of all UN officials and not just those working in human rights programs. The Human Rights Up Front program sought to ensure that protecting human rights was an integral part of the UN's work in all countries. UN offices around the globe must undertake risk analyses about the likelihood that atrocities would take place in their country and adjust the UN's work to manage that risk. At UN headquarters in New York, senior officials would conduct monthly regional reviews searching for warning signs of atrocity crimes. If serious concerns were identified, a warning would be sent to the UN's senior leadership, who would consider the emerging threat. If necessary, a warning would then be sent to the executive committee for the secretary-general and his senior advisors to review. The goal was to break down the silos within the UN that exist between the three core tasks of peace and security, development, and human rights. The Human Rights Up Front plan represented a broad cultural shift in the UN that emphasized the centrality of human rights in all UN work and underscored the importance of demonstrating moral courage.[17]

Eliasson and Gilmour presented the proposed plan to Secretary-General Ban Ki-moon, who accepted it and then went before the Security Council on November 22, 2013, to take ownership of it with what he called a commitment statement. Ban acknowledged the UN had not always effectively advocated for human rights and cited the debacle in Sri Lanka as an egregious failure. "Only by meeting our Charter responsibilities can the UN and its member states prevent horrendous human suffering. We can and must improve how we react to impending catastrophes. A coherent United Nations, exercising its moral and political responsibility and taking early civilian action, can have a transformational impact in preventing and ending gross violations of human rights and humanitarian law."[18]

Eliasson briefed the Security Council about a month later to explain the UN's renewed commitment to human rights in more detail. He acknowledged that the UN failed in the 1990s when it did little to prevent atrocities in Somalia, Rwanda, and Bosnia, adding that people in peril expect the UN to act. "However, in practice our response to crisis often comes when a situation has deteriorated to the point where only substantial political or peacekeeping missions can deal with the problems."

The premise of the Human Rights Up Front program was early and effective response to threats to human rights. UN headquarters would take a more proactive and coherent approach to coordinating the organization's response to potential crises. It would better organize staff and offices to alert member states of situations with a risk of serious abuses and violations of humanitarian law and share information on threats and risks.

There was an urgent need, Eliasson said, for more effective communication between the General Assembly, Security Council, and Human Rights Council. "We aim to respond and act as 'One UN,'" he pledged.[19]

Eliasson said serious human rights violations are the best early warning of impending atrocities—a fact that is too often ignored or not understood. "If we fail to act early, the human, political, and economic costs can be devastating as we know far too well." Eliasson added that the UN needed to build a more effective partnership with member states to protect human rights.

Enter Helen Clark, the director of the UN Development Program, and one of the highest-ranking UN officials. She supervised top UN officials in more than a hundred member nations. Though she was a crucial player to the new plan, Clark was widely believed to be cool to the initiative because it might lessen her autonomy. However, Eliasson persuaded her that they should send a joint letter describing the Human Rights Up Front program to the top UN officials in each country seeking their support.

They explained that the plan would allow the UN to leverage its mandates to help protect people at risk or subject to serious violations of international human rights or humanitarian law. They urged UN leaders in each country to pay close attention to human rights. "You are in a unique position to recognize changing events on the ground, to use your effective working relationships to understand the concerns of national counterparts and to recognize the vibrations caused by human rights violations that serve as early indicators of a deteriorating situation."

Eliasson and Clark pressed UN officials in the field to closely monitor and advocate for human rights in their jurisdictions and to reach out to headquarters in New York if more help were needed. They said a more intense focus on human rights reflected the best of the UN and its Charter. "Let's make it a reality in our day-to-day work," they implored.[20]

Eliasson believed the Human Rights Up Front program could play a key role in changing attitudes and reinserting human rights into the lifeblood of the UN. He told UN staff that if they were vigilant on human rights, he would back them up at headquarters. "I want UN staff to know that when they stick their necks out; when they give those early warning signals; whey they show courage; they should always be recognized, even rewarded, and we will back them up fully. This is an assurance that the secretary-general and I give," Eliasson vowed.[21]

During his time as deputy secretary-general, Eliasson worked valiantly to implement this program. He believed it could lead to much-needed changes with the UN: (1) a cultural change—alerting staff about the importance of preventing human rights abuses; (2) an operational change—to ensure that the UN better coordinate development, humanitarian, political, and human rights entities and actors; and (3) a communication change—emphasizing that member states are ultimately responsible for human rights within their jurisdictions.

Speaking at the General Assembly in January 2016, Eliasson reaffirmed the importance of the fledgling program. "Prevention is the fundamental premise and vocation of Human Rights Up Front," he said. "This initiative is an example of what we can do concretely to live up to the imperative of prevention." It aimed to help the United Nations operate in a more cohesive, crosscutting, and horizontal manner. Somewhat defensively, he said the program was "designed to be as informal and light as possible. . . . It does not involve any new reporting. Rather, it is a new approach and dimension to the work that we are already doing."[22]

As his term as deputy secretary-general was ending, Eliasson expressed hope that the new secretary-general, António Guterres, would continue and expand his hard-earned initiative.

THE FLICKERING FLAME OF HUMAN RIGHTS

When Guterres became secretary-general in January 2017, he vowed that advancing human rights would be a chief priority. However, his top legal advisor persuaded him to downplay the Human Rights Up Front initiative. Miguel de Serpa Soares, the UN's top legal advisor, had frequently differed with Eliasson on human rights issues. Eliasson believed the UN should aggressively and unabashedly embrace its role as the chief global protector of human rights. Serpa Soares evidently believed his job was to limit the UN's legal exposure on many issues, including human rights. He said the Human Rights Up Front plan duplicated the work of other UN bodies and was unnecessary. He argued that it also strained relations with member states, especially Russia and China. More than a year after Eliasson left the UN, Guterres closed the small unit in the Secretariat that oversaw the program and even rejected an offer from several Scandinavian governments to pay for it.

The decision greatly disappointed Eliasson, who had wanted to encourage and provide political support for UN workers in the field who challenged governments for human rights abuses.

Secretary-General Guterres was sharply criticized by the human rights community for downplaying these issues. Ken Roth, head of Human Rights Watch, wrote a scorching essay about the secretary-general in the *Washington Post* in the spring of 2019. He said Guterres was becoming defined by his silence on human rights, even as serious rights abuses proliferated. Roth acknowledged that all UN secretaries-general struggled to balance their role as judicious mediators of disputes with the need to advocate for fundamental UN values. "But for most rights issues, the dominant sound coming from the 38th floor of UN headquarters has been silence. There is no doubt that Guterres is a skilled and conscientious diplomat, but his decision to suppress his voice on human rights, especially as civilians are targeted in armed conflicts, is misguided."[23]

The secretary-general said that human rights advocacy was being absorbed into all the work of the UN. Perhaps stung by the criticism he received, Guterres created a new program he called "The Highest Aspiration: The Call for Action on Human Rights."[24] He also appointed a seasoned and respected UN official, Volker Turk, as the UN's High Commissioner for Human Rights.

Eliasson continues to believe the UN should remain in the forefront of advocating for the protection of human rights. Failing to do so diminishes the moral authority of the world body and imperils the lives of millions.

CHAPTER 5

Searching for Peace in Hell

IMPOSSIBLE NEGOTIATION

For a year and a half, Jan Eliasson, as the UN special envoy to Darfur, tried to find a way to end a years-long raging conflict. He was at the center of an extremely difficult, perhaps impossible, negotiation. He probed and pleaded with the government of Sudan, rebel leaders in the western region of Darfur, heads of neighboring countries, and the UN Security Council to help stop the fighting and begin negotiations.

He combined steadfast optimism with a professed, if not fully plausible, confidence that parties would come together and end the long and bloody war that was turning Darfur into a place of death and desolation.

However, Eliasson's skills in mediation and negotiation were rendered nearly irrelevant in the face of a plethora of obstacles:

- a divided Sudanese government
- fragmenting and multiplying rebel movements in Darfur that were more intent on securing power among themselves than finding an agreement with the Sudanese government
- a distracted and divided international community
- a UN Security Council that failed to develop clear and consistent policies toward Darfur

- meddlesome, mischievous, and sometimes mendacious regional powers who preferred to insinuate themselves into Darfur's struggles rather than ease or end them
- tribal and religious fissures in Darfur
- a fierce battle over scarce resources, including water and land between African farmers and Arab herders

During these eighteen months, Eliasson traveled thousands of miles, primarily in Europe and Africa. He dealt with skilled diplomats, intransigent generals, elderly tribal chiefs, embattled and often terrified humanitarian workers, and presidents and prime ministers more intent on survival and personal enrichment than in saving this beleaguered region. Throughout this diplomatic ordeal, Eliasson stubbornly embraced an optimistic outlook, citing incremental progress, anticipating diplomatic momentum, toiling for a breakthrough, and telling everyone who would listen that there was no military solution to the Darfur conflict, only a political one.

DARFUR IN FLAMES

The history of the conflict in Darfur is tragic and complicated. The region in western Sudan is about the size of Texas and its struggles emanate from, and are linked to, political turmoil and frequent bloodshed in Sudan.

Sudan was once the largest nation in Africa. It was unstable and violent even before it won its independence from the United Kingdom and Egypt in 1956. During the early years of the twenty-first century, war raged in Sudan between the largely Arab and Muslim North and the African and non-Muslim South. Intense international and regional diplomacy led to a tenuous peace agreement in 2005, which allowed the South to eventually hold a referendum about its future. In 2011 the South voted overwhelmingly to leave Sudan and establish a new country.[1] South Sudan came into existence that year, prematurely in the view of Eliasson, who did not believe its institutions were ready for nationhood.

But in 2003, as civil war raged between the northern and southern areas of Sudan, unrest also broke out in Darfur. Two rebel groups, the Sudan Liberation Army and the Justice and Equality Movement, sought greater autonomy for Darfur and redistribution of economic wealth and political power. In April 2003 rebels attacked the Al Fashir airport, destroying military equipment and striking the Sudanese army. Sudan's president, Omar al-Bashir, initially downplayed the attacks as small-scale banditry, but later responded fiercely. He ordered the Sudanese army to bomb Darfur from the air and enlisted local Arab militias to attack rebels, villages, and even civilians. Most terrifying were attacks by Arab militias called Janjaweed, or "evil horsemen," who ravaged villages and destroyed almost everything in their sight. Between 2003 and 2006, an estimated 300,000 Darfurians were killed and two million were displaced, from an overall population of six million.[2]

Darfur's horror was initially ignored by the international community as global leaders focused on negotiating a North-South agreement in Sudan. Some believed that confronting the unfolding tragedy in Darfur would derail their long quest to end the twenty-year civil war in Sudan. The UN Security Council showed scant interest in Darfur, saying almost nothing from 2003 until mid-2004.

UN Secretary-General Kofi Annan took an emergency trip to Darfur in July 2004 in an attempt to alert the world to the unfolding tragedy. He implored President al-Bashir to cease his brutal attacks in Darfur and negotiate with rebels. "We all agree that serious crimes are being committed," Annan said. Al-Bashir offered vague assurances to Annan, but he had a long record of making pledges to global leaders with no intention of honoring them. Jan Egeland, the UN's humanitarian coordinator, became deeply concerned about Darfur and traveled to the region several times. He described it as "one of the worst humanitarian crises in the world." In April 2004, Egeland briefed the UN Security Council, urging action to try to end the killing and chaos in Darfur. He repeated his plea several additional times until he stepped down from his post in late November 2006. The Security Council barely stirred.[3]

The world slowly woke up to the horror in Darfur as journalists chronicled the violence and suffering. Samantha Power wrote a powerful essay in the *New Yorker* in 2004 called "Dying in Darfur."[4] *New York Times* columnist Nicholas Kristof wrote a series of searing essays from, and about, Darfur, calling it "the most wretched place in the world today." He challenged America and the world community to end the suffering. Dozens of groups emerged to bring attention to the crisis and demand action. The Save Darfur Coalition was established in New York City in July 2004. It comprised hundreds of groups that sought to raise awareness about the atrocities. Celebrities such as George Clooney traveled to Darfur to highlight the suffering and call for an urgent global response.

A peace agreement was signed in May 2006 by the Sudanese government and one of the largest rebel groups. It was brokered by diplomats from the African Union, the United Nations, the United States, and the United Kingdom. The 115-page accord, known as the Abuja Peace Agreement, outlined compromises on national and state power sharing, demilitarizing the much-feared Janjaweed and other militias, integrating rebel forces into Sudan's army, promoting Darfur's economy, providing for a referendum on the future status of Darfur, and providing humanitarian aid to the region.[5]

From the outset, many questioned the agreement's effectiveness given that important groups in Darfur did not participate in the talks and Darfur's political and tribal leaders, civil society, and refugees were not consulted. Many saw it as an agreement imposed by international actors and accepted reluctantly by the Sudanese government. Just months after the agreement was announced, Jan Pronk, the UN special representative in Sudan, said it was effectively dead.

In November 2006 UN and African Union leaders jointly declared that "new momentum" was needed to end the violence in Darfur and to find a political solution to the conflict.

UN SPECIAL ENVOY
From September 2005 to September 2006, while serving as president of the UN General Assembly, Jan Eliasson decried the violence in Darfur and lamented the international community's quiescence. He helped pass a resolution in the General Assembly establishing the "Responsibility to Protect" doctrine in which the international community vowed to

intervene, when necessary and if approved by the Security Council, in the internal affairs of a country to stop atrocities. Commentators noted that for this doctrine to be taken seriously, it should guide the international's community's response to the tragedy in Darfur.[6]

Eliasson's presidency of the General Assembly concluded in September 2006, and his tenure as Sweden's foreign minister ended in October when his government was defeated in the national election. Eliasson returned to Stockholm and spent several weeks decompressing. But he was soon ready to consider a new challenge. Eliasson was honored when he was asked if he was interested in becoming the UN deputy secretary-general. But he had just spent five busy years in Washington, followed by a grueling year in New York, and it wasn't the right time to take on a full-time UN job outside of Sweden. Eliasson indicated that he would be open to other assignments if he could be based in Stockholm.

Several months later, Kofi Annan, in the final months of his UN tenure, called Eliasson and asked if he would serve as the UN special envoy to Darfur as part of the renewed diplomatic effort to end the war. He gently reminded Eliasson of some of his passionate statements about the suffering in Darfur. Annan told Eliasson that his incoming successor, Ban Ki-moon, supported Eliasson in the new position.

Eliasson knew he would be taking on a brutally difficult diplomatic challenge in which failure was not only possible, but likely. He privately saw Darfur as "mission impossible." However, there were forces impelling him to accept the post. He was horrified by the suffering in Darfur and frustrated at the international community's failure to do more. This would be the ultimate diplomatic challenge and test of his skills. A successful mediation would catapult Eliasson to the highest ranks of diplomacy. By accepting the post, he would help his friend Kofi Annan conclude his UN service with an important initiative. Eliasson had worked on Sudanese issues since 1993 and knew President al-Bashir, as well as African Union leaders. He may have felt that if anyone could untie the diplomatic knot in Darfur, it would be him. After consulting his wife, he agreed. Eliasson's appointment as special envoy was announced in the final weeks of 2006.[7]

PLUNGING INTO CHAOS

Eliasson's eighteen months in the Darfur maelstrom consisted of complex, high-stakes diplomacy as the war raged on; villages were burned, leaders stonewalled, armed movements proliferated, international bureaucracy stalled, and thousands of innocent people were slaughtered. In the first months of his Darfurian diplomacy, more than sixty humanitarian vehicles were hijacked, fifty-six NGO staff were abducted and ultimately released, thirty-one aid convoys were ambushed and looted, and thirteen relief organizations were forced to relocate due to attacks.

He conducted his diplomacy with presidents, prime ministers, and foreign ministers in pinstripes, with tribal chieftains in flowing robes, and with rebel leaders in military khakis. The work took him to a dozen countries and was both mind-numbingly complex and strikingly simple. His overarching goals were to stop the fighting, persuade the rebel movements to decide what specifically they wanted, convince the Sudanese government in Khartoum to negotiate in good faith with the rebel movements, and determine whether regional and international leaders were willing to help end the conflict or, at the very least, do no harm. His ultimate goal was for the government in Khartoum and the rebel leaders in Darfur to stop fighting and to sit down and negotiate an agreement that focused on wealth, power sharing, and security.

However, to launch even this basic and essential negotiation he needed the Sudanese government, which was badly divided into North and South power centers, to determine what it could accept in Darfur. Then he had to find a way to stop the rebel movements in Darfur from fragmenting and fighting among themselves. As he did this, he sounded out the UN Security Council, whose fifteen members had differing views on Sudan and the crisis in Darfur. He tried to understand the views and diplomatic commitment of the African Union, which would be his main partner in Darfur. And he needed to understand the views, and enlist the cooperation of, countries in the region that had been involved in Darfur—not always constructively—for decades, including Chad, Eritrea, Ethiopia, Egypt, and Libya.

Eliasson's Darfur diplomacy began on January 1, 2007, when he called Ban Ki-moon on his first day as secretary-general. Eliasson had tracked down Ban's direct phone number from Sweden's foreign ministry and called him on New Year's Day. He learned it was the first call Ban received as secretary-general. Eliasson told him that he was ready to get to work on Darfur. Eliasson traveled to New York a few days later to meet Ban, other officials in the UN Secretariat, and diplomats from about twenty countries in what was known as the Darfur Contact Group. These were countries with a professed desire to stop the violence there. Eliasson then traveled to Addis Ababa, Ethiopia, the headquarters of the African Union, to meet with AU leaders including his new partner, Salim Ahmed Salim, a veteran diplomat from Tanzania. The work to end the conflict in Darfur was to be a joint UN-AU diplomatic effort. Eliasson and Salim then went to Sudan to meet with the president and foreign minister and request approval to begin talks with rebels and governmental leaders in Darfur.

Briefing the press in Khartoum on January 11, 2007, Eliasson conveyed optimism, determination, and hope. "I have now come back to Africa," he said triumphantly, recalling his previous work on the continent as the UN under-secretary-general for humanitarian affairs from 1992 to 1994, when he worked in Sudan and Somalia. "The fact that I am here is the sign of the engagement of the international community," he said, noting that his role as UN special envoy had been created by Kofi Annan, supported by Ban, and accepted by al-Bashir and Alpha Omare Konaré, the chair of the AU. Eliasson said he welcomed the chance to work again with the AU's envoy, Salim Ahmed Salim. "So, there will be a Salim-Eliasson team. I have worked very closely with Salim before."

Eliasson told reporters he had just met with President al-Bashir and other Sudanese senior officials. "I had fruitful and substantive conversations in a positive spirit. I think I can say we have established a good working relationship and I was very warmly received by the Sudanese government."[8]

Some diplomats called for inserting a peacekeeping force in Darfur, but Eliasson observed that first "there has to be a peace to keep." He was convinced there was no military solution to the conflict. Eliasson said he would know the parties were open to a political process when there was a clear reduction in violence. If the fighting remained at the same level, or intensified, it would be difficult to reach a political settlement. "So, I have pleaded with the leadership here that there is such a reduction of violence." Failure to stem violence soon would doom diplomacy and "then we run the risk of a Darfur tragedy, with Darfur nightmares continuing year after year." Eliasson said his primary job was in "the diplomatic sphere," to help secure a peace to preserve.

About six weeks into their diplomacy, Eliasson and Salim were hopeful and determined. At a briefing in the region, Eliasson said the secretary-general gave the Darfur crisis the highest priority and he and Salim were working as a team. "We may have a division of labor between us, and we might work separately sometimes, but we are working, and we will always be working, as a team."

Eliasson said the critical diplomatic work would have to take place on the ground in Darfur. "This problem is in Darfur; this problem is in Sudan. We want to have as much work done here as possible. . . . We will try to work as much as possible with Darfur as our base." He said that he and Salim would use the Darfur Peace Agreement (DPA) of 2006 as their starting point, but adjustments to that accord were on the table. He dismissed the two extreme positions—that the DPA was the final word and hence untouchable and that the DPA was worthless and needed to be jettisoned. "We have been assured during these talks—which are still continuing of course—that none of these extreme positions ought to be accepted. That leaves us diplomatic space that we will try to use," he said.[9]

Several months of intense talks with leaders in Khartoum, Darfur, and the region, ensued. In early June Eliasson and Salim presented what they called a road map for peace. It had three elements: stop other negotiations that had been springing up across the region and direct all negotiations through Eliasson and Salim; encourage Sudan's government and the rebel movements to decide what outcome they wanted; and then invite key parties to a peace conference that summer or fall.

Meanwhile, at the end of July the UN Security Council authorized the deployment of a UN-AU peace operation, with a hybrid force of 26,000, to stem the bloodshed. However, the actual deployment of this force was blocked by the government of Sudan.

In late July and early August, Eliasson and Salim held talks in Tanzania with Darfurian rebel leaders, seeking their list of specific goals. They persuaded several to agree on a common agenda for the upcoming peace talks with the Sudanese government. The agenda included power sharing and enhanced representation for Darfur in Sudan, a fairer distribution of income from oil production, compensation for the 2003–2005 genocide in Darfur, and enhanced security in Darfur by disarming the Janjaweed, ending arms transfers to them, and demobilizing rebel soldiers.

The stage was set for a peace conference in Libya in late October 2007.

MOMENT OF TRUTH

Eliasson envisioned the peace conference and its preparation as a critical opportunity to generate diplomatic momentum. He would have preferred the talks not take place in Libya given the mercurial nature of its leader, Muammar Gaddafi. However, the AU leadership pressed hard for the location. Eliasson consulted Ban and they decided it was not worth endangering the talks over the venue of the conference. Eliasson came to regret this decision.

Eliasson was troubled by a surge in violence in Darfur before the talks, seeing this as a test of whether the parties were serious about a diplomatic settlement. "Now is the time for everyone to be in the same place," Eliasson said before the conference began, adding there was a "very grave responsibility" resting upon the rebel movements and the Sudanese government to participate in the talks, which he described as "the moment of truth" for Darfur. Eliasson was growing increasingly concerned that many of the key players were poised to boycott the negotiations. He gave assurances that the many rebel movements didn't have to settle all the differences between them before the talks began. "We will allow plenty of time for the movements to have consultations among themselves because the real negotiations will start only after we have had the full preparation of the parties."[10]

The peace talks in Sirte, Libya, were a debacle. Leaders of the key rebel movements boycotted the conference. President al-Bashir left before the conference began—hardly a signal that he took the talks seriously. Gaddafi ignored Eliasson's request that he give *brief* welcoming remarks. Instead, he delivered a lengthy, disjointed, and gloomy opening statement that discussed the 1648 Peace of Westphalia and the 1992 Los Angeles riots in the aftermath of the Rodney King beating. Gaddafi lamented the absence of key movement leaders, saying without them they could not achieve peace. The war in Darfur, he declared, should be solved by Sudan and other Africans and not the international community.

Eliasson was stunned and deflated by Gaddafi's remarks, which set a tone that was the complete opposite of what he had hoped. Then the designated rebel representative set aside the approved and vetted draft statement and instead blasted the government in Sudan. "I can't tell you how many promises they have broken," he said, dismissing Khartoum's announcement of a unilateral ceasefire.[11]

Trying to rescue the conference, Eliasson delivered the remarks of Secretary-General Ban, whose basic message was that it was a critical time for Darfur, observing that it had been almost a year and a half since the signing of the Darfur Peace Agreement and the situation had only deteriorated. "There is now an opportunity for peace through the political negotiations for which you have all gathered in Sirte today." Eliasson, speaking for Ban, said a robust peacekeeping force would help, but only political dialogue and inclusive consultations would yield a deal. "I urge all parties to commit to an immediate cessation of hostilities here and now."[12] Eliasson was disappointed that some movement leaders boycotted the talks, but added that "the door remains open, but if they continue to stay away, there is much they stand to lose." He argued that the issues should be discussed in Sirte, not elsewhere, and repeated there was no military solution, just a political one that would require "painful compromises" by all sides. Without political progress, the situation in Darfur could rapidly worsen and become even more intractable.

The Sirte peace talks limped along for weeks but Eliasson knew the process was unraveling. He insisted that it was possible to launch more substantive peace talks later in the year, but no one seemed convinced. Eliasson and Salim continued to meet with rebel movement leaders and intensified their outreach to the heads of government of Chad, Eritrea, Libya, and Egypt. Eliasson also hoped to aggressively bring Darfur's civil society into the peace process. "We have to do something different," he concluded.

Eliasson's one-year contract as UN special envoy in Darfur expired in January 2008. He agreed to extend it for six months, but he was deeply frustrated by the continuing stalemate. Further complicating matters were reports that al-Bashir was going to be indicted soon by the International Criminal Court for his policies toward Darfur. This ended his cooperation with the international community. Eliasson and Salim decided their diplomacy had run its course and both resigned in early June 2008. They held briefings about the stalemate in Darfur with the AU leadership on June 12 and with the UN Security Council two weeks later.

PARTING WORDS

Eliasson took the lead before the UN Security Council and prepared his remarks carefully. He sought to establish the historical context for the conflict in Darfur, explain the UN-AU diplomatic strategy to break the deadlock, examine why their efforts failed, and outline how the international community should deal with the continuing tragedy. He was determined to use his withdrawal statement to clarify issues and describe the way ahead as clearly as possible. Eliasson chose to give a very detailed account of his diplomacy in Darfur in order to underscore the gravity of the situation and to make clear to the Security Council that it needed to take a much more active role in pressuring parties and bringing the conflict to an end.

Eliasson explained that he and Salim began their Darfur diplomacy in late 2006 when the UN and AU agreed that new energy and fresh perspectives were needed in the aftermath of the failure of the Darfur Peace Agreement to solve key issues or end the unrest. He recalled his first Security Council briefing in March 2007 when he detected "a sense of deep fatigue and deep frustration on all sides following four years of conflict and suffering in Darfur." Eliasson said he knew then that the diplomatic challenge would be difficult, but he and Salim believed there was a window of opportunity and the potential for dialogue between the parties. He recalled their many visits to the region, urging the parties to halt the violence, improve security, address humanitarian emergencies, and launch a political process.

He described trips to rebel-controlled areas in Darfur, urging the various movements to unify and decide what they wanted from the government in Khartoum as it pertained to power and wealth sharing, and security. He also recalled meetings with Sudanese leaders in Khartoum and Juba, the capital of the South, and implored them to show military restraint and offer compromises to aid the political process in Darfur.

Eliasson said he detected progress in the summer of 2007, and he had hoped the October peace conference in Libya would yield positive results. However, the absence of key rebel movement leaders and of a consolidated Sudanese delegation made it extremely difficult to engage in substantive talks. The conditions were not ripe for fruitful negotiations. Eliasson lamented that the situation in Darfur had deteriorated since the peace conference. Violence continued and clashes between Sudan and its neighbor Chad imperiled a future peace in Darfur. Conflicts between the movements and the Sudanese army and among tribal militias made it clear, Eliasson said, "that this intractable conflict is still unfolding." He said the "security situation in Darfur should now be our primary concern." Eliasson regretted the "troubled state of affairs in the political process." The parties had not held substantive talks since the Sirte conference seven months earlier. Fragmentation within the rebel movements continued to affect their cohesion and preparedness for talks and they had a "great and genuine lack of trust in the government of Sudan."

Eliasson analyzed why the conflict in Darfur was so difficult to resolve and concluded that it required progress in four areas: Darfur, Sudan, the region, and the international community. This reflected the complex new global chessboard of the twenty-first century. Achieving peace in Darfur, Eliasson declared, required progress on multiple fronts in addition to the need for the rebel movements to unify, or at least come up with a common platform, to negotiate with Khartoum. The international community, especially the UN Security Council, had to intensify efforts to stop the war. The region was aflame, and he was certain there would be no peace in Darfur without normal relations between Sudan and Chad. The joint UN-AU security force needed to be fully deployed without interference from Sudan. The surge of arms in Darfur had to be slowed. Civil society, traditional leaders, representatives of the millions who had been displaced in Darfur had to become more involved. "I often quote the old Swedish saying that you can bring a horse to a waterhole but can't force him to drink," Eliasson said. "In the case of Darfur, there is now reason to seriously question whether the parties are ready to sit down at the negotiation table and make the compromises necessary for peace. Mr. Salim and I have tried our best to assist them."

Eliasson said he and Salim supported a new envoy who would take over and deserved the support of the international community. "The outside world, as much as the parties, has a responsibility to bring an end to this tragedy. For over five years, millions of people have suffered enormously. This simply cannot go on." Eliasson concluded by urging continued efforts. "I believe it is important for us not to fall into despair and passivity. We have been in the field, we have seen women crying out for water, we have seen kids dying more or less in front of us, we have seen the despair in the eyes of the people."

He urged a realistic approach, focused on ending the hostilities and creating a credible political process in which diplomacy could come to the fore.[13]

TRAGEDY WITHOUT END

Eliasson's experience in Darfur was searing, exasperating, and discouraging. An accomplished diplomat, he could not entice the parties into serious negotiation. A skilled mediator, he could not get the parties to decide what they wanted and to sit down to reach an accord. "My main goal was to bring the main parties together to negotiate," he later recalled. Eliasson was also deeply frustrated that key members of the UN Security Council refused to use their power and influence to help end the war in Darfur. He believed, for example, that China had significant influence over the government of Sudan but declined to use it to force intense and good faith negotiations by Khartoum.

Eliasson is widely credited with doing his best in Darfur, but he has not escaped criticism. Julie Flint, a journalist who specializes in Sudan, wrote a hard-hitting report in 2010 about the failure to bring peace to

Darfur. She was critical of the Sudanese government, rebel movements, and the international community, including its various mediators and special envoys. She did not spare Eliasson and Salim.

She said that in their desire to be inclusive, they accommodated marginal rebel groups who did not deserve to be there. "Without clear criteria for allocating seats at the negotiating table, the envoys alienated the most important rebel leaders and made unification unattractive." Flint believed that Eliasson and Salim did not reach out creatively and effectively to civil society in Darfur such as tribal leaders, refugees, and women. She faulted them for not working full-time in the region and cites unnamed aides who said that both envoys had other projects going on simultaneously and were not fully focused on Darfur. She argues that the Sirte conference was a disaster that failed because of a lack of careful preparation in which the key parties were either not there or not ready to have meaningful negotiations.[14]

Eliasson's time in Darfur was a dispiriting lesson in the reality of proxy wars—in which outside powers fuel the conflict, use it to fight their own battles, and then intrude in the peace process. He looks back with sadness and is stricken by the endless suffering and bloodshed in Darfur and Sudan.

He is still searching for the best way to think about his work in Darfur. "It was of course not a success. Was it a failure? I don't know. We did what we could. Perhaps we offered ideas that will one day bear fruit. That is my hope." He is horrified that the tragedy in Sudan and Darfur intensified in 2023 and shows no signs of resolution. "It's a forgotten conflict. It continues in the shadow of Ukraine, of Yemen, of the consequences of climate change."

Eliasson meets with Sweden's Crown Princess Victoria during her visit to the United Nations. Eliasson served as an informal mentor to Victoria. (J. Countess/WireImage)

Eliasson, brandishing a copy of the UN Charter, speaks before a concert in the UN General Assembly Hall. He kept a copy in his suit pocket. (Kena Betancur/Getty Images)

Eliasson attends an awards dinner with his wife, Kerstin. (Vanessa Marisak/Getty Images)

Eliasson, holding a glass of water, his trademark gesture, to underscore the importance of water and sanitation issues at a UN event in New York. (Larry Busacca/Getty Images)

Eliasson, as the UN's special envoy for Darfur, exchanges a few words with an African Union soldier in Darfur. (Isam Al-Haj/AFP via Getty Images)

Eliasson and UN Secretary-General Kofi Annan speak before a UN meeting in New York. (Stan Honda/AFP via Getty Images)

Eliasson joins as a Sudanese healer prays for his peace efforts in a marketplace in Darfur. (Carolyn Cole/Los Angeles Times via Getty Images)

Eliasson consults with Gerard McHugh, a UN military expert, while traveling in Darfur to meet with tribal leaders. (Carolyn Cole/Los Angeles Times via Getty Images)

Eliasson confers with his predecessor as president of the UN General Assembly, Jean Ping of Gabon, during a UN meeting. (Mike Nagle/Getty Images)

Eliasson addresses the UN Security Council as Samantha Power, the US ambassador to the United Nations, reviews her briefing materials. (Albin Lohr-Jones/Pacific Press/LightRocket via Getty Images)

Eliasson speaks to students at a school for Syrian child refugees in Lebanon. (Bilal Jawich/Anadolu Agency/Getty Images)

Eliasson, UN Secretary-General Ban Ki-moon, and director-screenwriter Richard Curtis observe projections of the 17 Sustainable Development Goals on the UN General Assembly Building. (Kena Betancur/Getty Images for Global Goals)

CHAPTER 6

The Quest for Sustainable Development

TIME OF CELEBRATION

The third week of September 2015 was a joyful time at the United Nations. More than 150 global leaders gathered in New York City to attend festivities celebrating its seventieth anniversary and to approve an ambitious plan called "Transforming our World: The 2030 Agenda for Sustainable Development." This plan contained the seventeen Sustainable Development Goals (SDGs), which had been laboriously developed, negotiated, and fine-tuned over three years and was the most ambitious global development plan world leaders had ever considered. To mark the occasion, the UN planned a multiday event with musical performances by the Colombian singer Shakira, testimonials by hundreds of young people, and remarks by Pope Francis. The UN building was lit up for several days with the SDG logo and a film about them playing in a loop on an exterior wall. New York City taxi drivers even provided mini tutorials about the seventeen SDGs in a video that played on Taxi TV.[1]

On September 25, Pope Francis spoke to global leaders at the UN General Assembly before it formally approved the SDGs. The pontiff told the rapt audience that adoption of the 2030 Agenda on Sustainable Development was "'an important sign of hope." But he also offered words of caution. "Solemn commitments, however, are not enough, even though they are a necessary step toward solutions." The pope warned of the limitations of the "bureaucratic exercise of drawing up long lists of good proposals—goals, objectives, and statistical indicators." He urged policymakers to always be aware that their actions affected "real men and women who live, struggle and suffer, and are often forced to live in great poverty, deprived of all rights."[2]

Secretary-General Ban Ki-moon then described the SDGs in sweeping terms. "We have reached a defining moment in human history. The people of the world have asked us to shine a light on a future of promise and opportunity," he declared. "The new agenda is a promise by leaders to all people everywhere. It is a universal, integrated, and transformative vision for a better world. It is an agenda for people, to end poverty in all its forms. An agenda for the planet, our common home. An agenda for shared prosperity, peace, and partnership." However, the secretary-general acknowledged that turning the seventeen goals into a transformed world would be a demanding challenge. "The true test of the commitment to Agenda 2030 will be implementation. We need action from everyone, everywhere. The 2030 Agenda compels us to look beyond national boundaries and short-term interests and to act in service of the long term."[3]

Deputy Secretary-General Jan Eliasson was not at center stage for the approval of the SDGs, but he was watching closely in the hall, relishing the moment and accomplishment. He had played a quietly constructive role in this drama. For many years he had repeatedly urged global and national leaders to complete work on an earlier set of global goals, the Millennium Development Goals (MDGs), which paved the way for this successor plan, the Sustainable Development Goals. Eliasson praised the MDGs, while acknowledging their limitations.

Eliasson was part of Ban Ki-moon's leadership team and helped shape several of the SDGs. He worked closely with two UN officials, Amina Mohammed and David Nabarro. Eliasson focused especially on goals that dealt with the need for clean water and better sanitation, and preserving the health of the world's oceans. He also championed a goal pertaining to the need for effective governance and stronger local and global institutions. He helped push the SDGs through the UN's complex and cumbersome bureaucratic process: briefing diplomats, making phone calls, sending notes, and discussing the new agenda in formal and informal meetings. He was one of the UN's most persistent and eloquent champions of the SDGs, extolling them to dozens of audiences as they were fashioned, and then agreed to, by global leaders. Finally, he intensely focused on implementing the seventeen goals, steadfastly refusing to declare victory once they were formally approved in September 2015. Follow-through was everything.

Eliasson's work on the SDGs underscores the reality that diplomats are often not the originators or architects of grand plans, but play an essential role as negotiators, advocates, champions, and storytellers. Eliasson describes the SDGs as part of a complex diplomatic agenda that came to fruition in 2015, an agenda that included separate, but related, negotiations on development finance, disaster risk reduction, and climate change.

MILLENNIUM DEVELOPMENT GOALS

Throughout its history, the UN has championed poverty reduction and environmental stewardship but often as separate, and sometimes competing, initiatives. Since it began operating in 1946, it has fought to end poverty and since the 1970s it has focused on preserving the environment. The UN hosted an important environmental conference in 1972 in Stockholm and the 1983 Brundtland Commission that pioneered the concept of sustainable development with its landmark report, "Our Common Future." At the 1992 Earth Summit in Rio de Janeiro, more than 175 countries adopted Agenda 21, a comprehensive plan to forge a global partnership for sustainable development to improve living standards in an environmentally safe way.[4]

As the year 2000 approached, UN Secretary-General Kofi Annan decided to center the Millennium Summit on a commitment to alleviate extreme poverty in the world. This commitment was encapsulated in the Millennium Declaration endorsed by global leaders in September 2000. This declaration led to the eight Millennium Development Goals (MDGs) to reduce extreme poverty by 2015. The actual MDGs were written hurriedly in a UN office by aides to Annan, drawing on the language and rhetorical commitments made in earlier global agreements. To the surprise of many, the MDGs captured the attention of policymakers and business leaders across the world.

The eight goals were simple and could be placed on a poster or chart:

Goal 1: Eradicate extreme poverty and hunger

Goal 2: Achieve universal primary education

Goal 3: Promote gender equality and empower women

Goal 4: Reduce child mortality

Goal 5: Improve maternal health

Goal 6: Combat HIV/AIDS, malaria, and other diseases

Goal 7: Ensure environmental sustainability

Goal 8: Develop a global partnership for development

The MDGs also included twenty-one subgoals, known as targets, all of which were hoped to be achieved by 2015.[5]

Jeffrey Sachs, an economist who helped create the MDGs, argued that they marked a "historic and effective method of global mobilization to achieve a set of important social priorities worldwide. . . . By packaging these priorities into an easily understandable set of eight goals, and by establishing measureable and time-bound objectives, the MDGs promote global awareness, political accountability, improved metrics, social feedback and public pressures."[6] Bill Gates, the entrepreneur and philanthropist, called them a global report card in the fight against poverty.

The MDGs appeared successful. During this period, there was a dramatic reduction in global poverty, although many observed this was largely attributable to robust economic growth in China and India. Between 2000 and 2015 about three hundred million people in each of the two countries emerged out of extreme poverty. However, this poverty reduction strategy paid little attention to environmental or social concerns. The MDGs did shape the global conversation on poverty and development. Their targets were specific, actionable, and measurable. They were not legally binding but had strong political and moral weight. They stood in stark contrast to the unwieldy output of the 1992 Rio

Earth Summit, which produced a 350-page report with 115 programmatic initiatives.

Critics said the MDGs had significant limitations, with some ridiculing them as *Minimum* Development Goals. Skeptics noted that they were written by officials in the secretary-general's office with little input from the member states or other institutions within the UN system. The MDGs focused on what the developing world could do to emerge from poverty. Some believed they delivered a patronizing message in which the Global North told the Global South what it should do. Other skeptics said each of the eight goals was seen as a separate and specific challenge with little sense of connection or synergy. Still, many global leaders, diplomats, and development experts viewed the MDGs as a striking success in setting a tangible development agenda and asserted that the discipline of setting global goals was a constructive, innovative step in international diplomacy.

MDGs TO SDGs

In July 2010, Ban Ki-moon created the Millennium Development Goals Advocacy Panel to explain and promote the MDGs to as many audiences as possible. It comprised development experts and global leaders including Jan Eliasson, who had left the UN and was living in Stockholm. The panel first met in Madrid to consider how to rally global support to achieve the MDGs, which were set to expire in five years. Eliasson spoke to stakeholders about the MDGs and was interviewed for a video in which he explained several goals.[7]

As 2015 approached, Ban and others in the UN began to discuss if the MDGs should be extended or whether a new, broader set of goals, with environmental and social metrics, was necessary. Ban created several high-level panels to explore this issue as the UN began to prepare for the 2012 Rio+20 Summit, to pay tribute to the Brazilian city's landmark 1992 Earth Summit. Diplomats and development experts considered how the summit could update, and significantly expand, the MDGs. The Rio summit produced a report in June 2012 titled "The Future We Want," which reaffirmed the importance of the MDGs and called for an intense effort to reach the goals by 2015. It also called for a bolder future agenda by establishing an intergovernmental high-level political forum to begin work on new Sustainable Development Goals. The SDGs should be global, aspirational, action-oriented, concise, easy to communicate, limited in number, and applicable to all countries, while taking into account different national realities.

After Rio+20 the UN's bureaucratic processes revved up. The summit mandated an Open Working Group with thirty representatives of UN member states who were instructed to prepare a report on the SDGs for the General Assembly.

At the same time the secretary-general worked with member states to draft a paper to frame the SDG debate. That report, "A Life of Dignity for All," called for Sustainable Development Goals that focused on economic growth, social justice, and environmental stewardship. "This post 2015 framework can bring together the full range of human aspirations and needs to ensure a life of dignity for all," it declared. The MDGs had shown that much could be accomplished through a combination of targets, investments, political will, and global attention to end poverty. Leaders and nations should do all they could to achieve the MDGs by the end of 2015. However, it noted that the world had changed and a "new era demands a new vision and a responsive framework. Sustainable development . . . must become our global guiding principle and operational standard."[8]

Meanwhile, the Open Working Group held thirteen meetings between March 2013 and July 2014. It received ideas from governments and civil society and generated thousands of pages of proposals and explanations. The working group ultimately proposed 17 SDGs and 169 targets. After the General Assembly received this proposal, it launched a year-long negotiation that transformed the draft into a formal UN resolution that added a preamble and declaration to the goals and targets. The deliberations were led by Csaba Korosi of Hungary, David Donoghue of Ireland, and Macharia Kamau of Kenya. An agreement was reached on August 2, 2015, after several all-night negotiations. Less than two months later the UN General Assembly approved the SDG plan on September 25, 2015.

ELIASSON CHAMPIONS THE SDGS

Eliasson followed the UN's complex deliberations and draft proposals of the Sustainable Development Goals closely. As a private citizen who was a member of the high-profile MDG Advocacy Group, he was convinced of the value of global goal setting and that the MDGs were an important project that should guide the global development agenda through 2015.

Once back at the UN as deputy secretary-general, Eliasson had a more public role. In the fall of 2012, he spoke to multiple groups about the importance of the MDGs—and the need to continue to press hard to reach its goals by 2015. "We should never forget that we still have work to do on the present Millennium Development Goals," he said that October. He added that much had been accomplished but renewed energy was needed and there were "grave deficiencies in the achievement of these goals." He cited the goals pertaining to maternal health and sanitation, admonishing that regarding sanitation "it is almost scandalous that so little is going to be achieved."[9]

Speaking about six weeks later, Eliasson argued that completing the unfinished work of the MDGs by 2015 should be the top priority, while recognizing that "the Millennium Development Goals are a staging post on a longer road." Work was already underway on a post-2015 development agenda, the SDGs, and he said the new plan should tackle issues not covered by the MDGs such as growing inequality, unsustainable consumption and production patterns, changing population dynamics, migration, urbanization, the digital divide, rule of law, governance, and accountability at all levels. The central challenge was addressing these development needs without ending up with a long list of goals. "Such an approach would only weaken the agenda. Length is not the right measure of comprehensiveness. We must avoid ending up with rhetorical declarations or a negotiations process characterized by identifying lowest common denominators." He added that the coming months would be hard and challenging yet also exciting. "We have a tremendous opportunity," he said. "Let us remember that our measure of success is the difference our work makes for the lives of the people of the world were are to help and serve."[10]

Throughout 2013 Eliasson continued to call for acceleration of work to meet the MDGs while actively contemplating the new agenda. Speaking to a Washington think tank, Eliasson acknowledged that the current SDGs draft included too many goals but added that this was the preference of the UN membership. He underscored that setting ambitious goals is a different challenge than meeting them. "The 'what' is easy. The 'how' is difficult. I've been mainly dealing with the 'how.'"

His 2014 work with Ban and a key UN official, Amina Mohammed, would lead to a report from the secretary-general that would contribute to negotiations on the SDGs. Though not legally binding, the final report would carry weight. "The power of the agenda lies in its ability to inspire, guide, and persuade. For this we must realize that good international solutions to global challenges are in the national interest," Eliasson said.[11]

In July 2015 Eliasson addressed the UN High-level Political Forum on sustainable development and delivered his most comprehensive and nuanced remarks on the emerging SDGs the UN would consider in a few months. He said that he hoped history would see 2015 as a "turning point—when the path shifted trajectory towards a future where men, women, and children around the world were given a chance to live their lives in dignity on a safe planet." He said that the legacy passed on to our children and grandchildren would depend on whether the agenda adopted at the September summit was ambitious and transformational and adhered to.

The new agenda needed to be based on synergies between the goals; he added that a weakness of the MDGs was that they focused on discrete goals rather that the relationships between them. "One of the lessons from the MDGs is that we cannot work in silos. Focusing on one goal, without considering the links to other goals, is not optimal. That is why we need an integrated vision of implementation, in which interlinkages are well understood and utilized." He warned that the path ahead was daunting, saying "substantially transforming societies and economies on a global scale is not a road we have travelled before. We need more than a new toolbox of policy measures. We need an essential 'rethink' of the way we make and implement policies." Global leaders needed to be both visionary and practical. "We have a grave and commanding responsibility to advance a model for development for the next fifteen years. We must embrace the path charted by this agenda towards transformation, prosperity and dignity for all on a healthy planet."[12]

On September 24, the day before world leaders approved the SDGs at the UN, Eliasson addressed a seminar for business leaders and academics in New York City. He said that after initial hesitation from some quarters there was great excitement and anticipation around the seventeen Sustainable Development Goals that were the centerpiece of the 2030 agenda. Accomplishing these goals would require the support of governments, business, civil society, and individuals. "This is a mission supremely worth embarking upon, in the pursuit of a life of dignity for all and of a healthy planet with which we live in peace and harmony."[13]

SUPPORTERS AND SKEPTICS

The UN approved the SDGs amidst great fanfare with global leaders extolling their benefits. President Barack Obama spoke before the world body on September 27 and declared, "I am committing the United States to achieving the Sustainable Development Goals." However, he added, "The question before us, though, as an international community, is how do we meet these new goals that we've just set today? How can we do our work better? How can we stretch our resources and our funding more effectively? How can donor countries be smarter and how can recipient countries do more with what they receive?"[14]

The Sustainable Development Goals are presented below:

1. End poverty in all its forms everywhere

2. End hunger, achieve food security and improved nutrition and promote sustainable agriculture

3. Ensure healthy lives and promote well-being for all at all ages

4. Ensure inclusive and equitable quality education and promote lifelong learning opportunities for all

5. Achieve gender equality and empower all women and girls

6. Ensure availability and sustainable management of water and sanitation for all

7. Ensure access to affordable, reliable, sustainable and modern energy for all

8. Promote sustained, inclusive and sustainable economic growth, full and productive employment and decent work for all

9. Build resilient infrastructure, promote inclusive and sustainable industrialization and foster innovation

10. Reduce inequality within and among countries

11. Make cities and human settlements inclusive, safe, resilient and sustainable

12. Ensure sustainable consumption and production patterns

13. Take urgent action to combat climate change and its impacts

14. Conserve and sustainably use the oceans, seas and marine resources for sustainable development

15. Protect, restore and promote sustainable use of terrestrial ecosystems, sustainably manage forests, combat desertification, and halt and reverse land degradation, and halt biodiversity loss

16. Promote peaceful and inclusive societies for sustainable development, provide access to justice for all and build effective, accountable and inclusive institutions at all levels

17. Strengthen the means of implementation and revitalize the Global Partnership for Sustainable Development.[15]

Despite their support within the UN, the SDGs faced skepticism even before they were approved in September 2015. That March, as work on the SDGs intensified, *The Economist* magazine ripped into the emerging plan, saying that the 17 goals and 169 targets demonstrated what happens when a bureaucratic process spins out of control. "Moses brought ten commandments down from Mount Sinai. If only the UN's proposed list of Sustainable Development Goals were as concise. The SDGs are supposed to set out how to improve the lives of the poor in emerging countries, and how to steer money and government policy toward areas where they can do the most good. But the efforts of the SDG drafting committees are so sprawling and misconceived that the entire enterprise is being set up to fail. That would be not just a wasted opportunity, but also a betrayal of the world's poorest people." *The Economist* called the SDGs "a mess" and estimated that meeting them would cost between $2 and $3 trillion a year of public and private money over fifteen years, a sum that would never be secured.[16]

William Easterly, a prominent development economist, wrote a withering assessment of the SDGs in *Foreign Policy* titled, "The SDGs Should Stand for Senseless, Dreamy and Garbled." He cited another analyst who dismissed them as a "high school wish list on how to save the world." He compared the SDGs unfavorably to the MDGs, saying the MDGs were appealing because they were precise and measurable and the SDGs are "so encyclopedic that everything is a top priority, which means nothing is a priority." He seized on the SDGs utopian language and noted they are offered not as ideals but targets for 2030. "So, the SDGs are to monitor the attainment of goals that cannot be monitored or attained, financed by unidentified financing."[17]

SURVIVAL KIT FOR HUMANITY

Eliasson argues the SDGs are a historic accomplishment. Drawing on a discussion with Johan Rockström, a Swedish expert on global sustainability issues, Eliasson calls the SDGs a "toolbox for repairing the world," and "a survival kit for humanity." He refers to them as a "21st century Declaration of Interdependence." He also describes the SDGs as the blueprint to implement the Paris Climate Accords.

However, Eliasson has long insisted that for the SDGs implementation is everything. Speaking in February 2016 to the Organisation for Economic Co-operation and Development in Paris, Eliasson urged a "whole of-society, whole-of-government strategy, involving all levels of government, as well as other partners" to implement the new goals.

"With the SDGs, we have—together—a unique chance to make poverty history, to tangibly improve peoples' lives and to stop the degradation of the environment. In spite of many troubling trends in the world, we must make the next fifteen years a turning point in human history. Each and every one of us has a responsibility to translate the Sustainable Development Goals into realities."[18] He remained steadfast on the importance of implementation. Speaking five months later at a UN event he urged, "Let us be under no illusion: the implementation path will not be easy. Achieving the SDGs is a monumental task."[19]

At one of his final press conferences as deputy secretary-general, in November 2016 Eliasson said the previous year had been a good one for multilateralism, citing international approval of the SDGs, the Paris Climate Accords, and two other lesser-known conferences, the Sendai Conference on disaster risk reduction, and the Addis Conference on financing for development.

Implementing the SDGs has been, as Eliasson warned, very difficult. Even under the best of circumstances, the agenda was going to be challenging. Moving from idealistic, even utopian, ideas to actually changing the world's economy and environment is a formidable, perhaps impossible, challenge.

Covid-19 descended on the world in early 2020 and caused massive economic and social disruptions, including a surge in poverty. Then Russia invaded Ukraine in February 2022 and that war has been both disruptive and tragic. There has also been a steady flow of natural disasters for global and national leaders to address.

Assessments of the status of the SDG project have not been encouraging. *The Political Impact of the Sustainable Development Goals* was published in 2022 by Frank Bierman, Thomas Hickman, and Carole-Anne Senit. It concludes that since 2015 the SDGs have created a strong set of normative guidelines but have not been a transformative force. It describes the scope of the 2030 agenda and the SDGs as unprecedented and says it "sets the bar high—possibly higher than it has ever been before, with ambitious goals." The authors conclude that the SDGs have been aspirational but have not steered governments, civil society, and corporations toward sustainable development. They have changed the language and conversation about global development, but they have not changed the policies and budgets of national governments and multilateral institutions. "There is little evidence that institutions are realigned, that funding for sustainable development is re-allocated, that policies are becoming more stringent, or that new and more demanding laws and programs are established because of the goals." Most troubling, the book questions if the SDGs might actually be hampering real reforms by "providing a smokescreen of hectic political activity that blurs a reality of stagnation, dead ends and business as usual." It questions whether the goals allow international organizations, governments, and corporations to "merely pretend to be taking decisive action to address the concerns of citizens while clinging to the status quo."[20]

Reports by the UN have also raised hard-hitting questions about the effect of the SDGs. In the summer of 2023, at the midpoint of the SDG's fifteen-year time frame, the UN released several reports that starkly acknowledged the goals are far off track. "The Sustainable Development Goals are disappearing in the rearview mirror—and with them the hope and rights of current and future generations. A fundamental shift is needed—in commitment, solidarity, financing, and action—to put the world on a better path. And it is needed now," according to one UN study. "'It's time to sound the alarm. . . . The SDGs are in deep trouble." It added that governments and the private sector and civil society must intensify work on all levels, including a sweeping effort to overhaul the global financial and economic system.[21]

The UN General Assembly approved a political declaration in September 2023 that urged an intensive global recommitment to the SDGs and linked this to reform of the international financial system so that substantially more capital is available and allocated for the goals.[22]

Eliasson acknowledges that the world has fallen behind schedule on the SDGs but believes this is partly due to the disruptions caused by the Covid-19 pandemic, the war in Ukraine, and inflationary pressures since 2021. "We can't give up or slow down on the SDGs. They are very important for our future, our survival," he says.

The Culture of Prevention

THE IMPERATIVE OF PREVENTION

The central theme of Jan Eliasson's long and consequential diplomatic career is the imperative of prevention. He is convinced that a great deal of the misery that has afflicted the world could have been prevented with foresight and action. He initially focused on prevention in the context of human rights abuses, but has expanded the concept to include climate change, pandemics, refugees and migrants, and extreme poverty.

Successful prevention requires effective early warning systems, robust response capacity, strong political will, and effective government and civil society responses. Eliasson believes the technical challenges of developing effective early warning and response systems are real but solvable. The most daunting challenge, however, is political will. Throughout history, political leaders have been reluctant to devote resources to confront problems that are looming but have not yet arrived. Additionally, the political rewards for preventing problems are minimal.

Eliasson is convinced that creating a culture of prevention is a historic challenge that is necessary and urgent.

SWEDEN EMBRACES PREVENTION

In 1998 Jan Eliasson, then Sweden's deputy foreign minister, met with the country's new foreign minister, Anna Lindh, to discuss Sweden's foreign policy agenda. Lindh, a rising star in Swedish politics, wanted to continue her country's foreign policy traditions while also finding a signature issue for her tenure as the leader of Swedish diplomacy. During their meeting, Eliasson recalled his experiences as the UN's first under-secretary-general for humanitarian affairs in the early 1990s when he saw, with his own eyes, heartbreaking humanitarian tragedies in Somalia, Sudan, Mozambique, the Balkans, and elsewhere. Eliasson's tenure left him with enduring memories, frustrations, and convictions. More than anything else, he became convinced that too many resources are spent, and too many lives are lost, trying to stop wars that have already started while too few resources are devoted to preventing them.

During his 1994 sabbatical at Uppsala University's Department of Peace and Conflict Research, Eliasson pondered what could be done to prevent so much destruction and suffering. He collaborated with Professor Peter Wallensteen, an expert in the field. The two men developed a diplomatic process they called the Ladder of Prevention.[1]

Their idea was to identify actions that could be taken by those who saw an impending conflict and were determined to prevent it from turning bloody and destructive. The Ladder of Prevention involved multiple steps beginning with deploying early warning systems. If that failed, the international community could conduct fact-finding missions, mediation, and arbitration, dispatch troops or observers, impose targeted sanctions, threaten the use of force, and—if no solution had been successful—use force. They later expanded this concept and defined it as the Pyramid of Prevention. It addressed situations where force was needed, and steps were required, to deescalate tensions and prevent future military conflict.

Lindh asked Eliasson to create a task force within the Swedish foreign ministry to develop a program on conflict prevention. She wanted to focus on the root causes of conflict, known as structural prevention, as well as on direct measures, often called operational prevention, to stop conflicts from turning violent or from recurring. Eliasson's task force built upon his previous work with Wallensteen to examine Sweden's experiences in international diplomacy, conflict resolution, international development cooperation, and peacekeeping. Eliasson recalls that during one task force discussion in early 1999, the term "a culture of prevention" was seized on, "indicating the importance of having prevention penetrate and permeate activities as well as attitudes in dealing with situations that could turn into conflict."

Sweden's foreign ministry worked with several other government agencies on a report that was released in 1999, "Preventing Violent Conflict: A Swedish Action Plan." Printed as a small yellow booklet, it contained big ideas and lofty aspirations. "Armed conflict and war must be prevented. The enormous human and financial resources used for destruction must be used for construction and development instead. It is necessary to ensure that armed conflicts and wars never break out," it declared. "We need to encourage new attitudes in diplomacy, international peace-promoting activities, and development co-operation. Thus, new norms and tools must be created and developed. Only by moving the focus from the late stages of crises to early warning signals of nascent conflicts can we at last make essential early action possible." The report argued that conflict prevention should become an integral part of Swedish foreign and security policy. It acknowledged that conflict prevention is difficult to do operationally and often has little political support because averted conflicts don't make headlines, aren't publicly visible, and don't engage people emotionally.[2]

The next year, Sweden's foreign ministry submitted an expanded version of the report to Parliament. "Preventing violent conflict at an early stage has never been a priority for the international community, despite recognition of the fact that it is better to prevent a conflict than to be forced to try to control it and, when that fails, to deal with the consequences," it said. "The international community in a broad sense—states, international and nongovernmental organizations, and other actors—must adopt a conflict prevention approach or what may be called a conflict prevention culture." It recognized the need for a paradigm shift, refocusing attention and resources from managing violent conflicts to preventing them. "Conflicts are a natural and inevitable part of normal political life in all societies, including democracies, and they often drive progress. The challenge for conflict prevention is to ensure that conflicts are managed in such a way to avoid violence and human suffering." The report considered the challenge of summoning political will to intervene, citing practical and psychological barriers. "There is a deep-rooted tendency to put off dealing with problems until they become acute."[3]

Sweden held the presidency of the European Union in 2001 and used its position to thrust conflict prevention into the EU's foreign policy agenda. The Prevention of Violent Conflict, an EU program adopted in June 2001, reflected Sweden's views on the importance of conflict prevention. EU officials, Eliasson recalled, supported the Swedish-backed initiative but remained somewhat skeptical.[4]

Several months later, the 9/11 terrorist attacks struck the United States and America launched the so-called War on Terror, which began in Afghanistan but soon shifted to the United States' preemptive war in Iraq. Anna Lindh was tragically murdered in Stockholm in 2002. A new Swedish government came to power in 2006 and placed less importance on the concept of prevention.

Although its visibility has waxed and waned, fostering a culture of prevention has remained a goal of Swedish foreign policy for more than two decades, in no small part because Eliasson has forcefully advocated for it and promoted the ideal. Others have joined him. In January 2017, Sweden chaired the UN Security Council and decided that the agenda for the first session with the new secretary-general, António Guterres, would focus on conflict prevention and sustaining peace. In a background memo for the UN Security Council debate, Swedish diplomat Olof Skoog called for a "new political consensus in support of prevention and a commitment to policies and actions that prevent conflict before they begin." The memo noted that too often the Security Council was seized with "addressing the crises of the day rather than preventing the conflicts of tomorrow." Adequately funded prevention programs could prevent conflict from occurring in the first place, saving lives and money, and protecting development gains.[5] Sweden's foreign minister, Margot Wallström, then made the same basic case for prevention before the UN that Eliasson had made two decades earlier within the Swedish government. "Can we afford an ever-growing list of crises slipping into violent conflict and needless human misery?" Wallström asked the Security Council. "What we need now is a new political consensus in support of prevention."[6]

PREVENTION AND THE UNITED NATIONS

Sweden's commitment to creating a culture of prevention has been shared by several other countries, nongovernmental organizations, the European Union, and the United Nations. The nomenclature has sometimes differed; the desire to prevent conflict and suffering has been variously called preventive diplomacy, conflict prevention, and the culture of prevention.

The most recent UN secretaries-general have embraced this aspiration. However, they have found it easier to summon language endorsing the concept than deploying practical tools to make it a reality. In 1992 Boutros Boutros-Ghali presented a sweeping report titled "An Agenda for Peace," with prevention at its heart. "Preventive diplomacy is action to prevent disputes from arising between parties, to prevent existing disputes from escalating into conflicts, and to limit the spread of the latter when they occur," he wrote. "The most desirable and efficient employment of diplomacy is to ease tensions before they result in conflict—or, if conflict breaks out, to act swiftly to contain it and resolve its underlying causes."[7] But there were few examples of effective prevention under his watch.

Kofi Annan, secretary-general from 1997 to 2006, was captivated by the concept of prevention. In a 1999 report, he made a compelling case. "Today, no one disputes that prevention is better and cheaper than reacting to crises after the fact. Yet our political and organizational cultures and practices remain oriented far more toward reaction than prevention. In the words of the ancient proverb, it is difficult to find money for medicine, but easy to find it for a coffin." Annan continued this theme the following year. "Yes, prevention costs money but intervention, relief, and rebuilding broken societies and lives costs far more. We must make conflict prevention the cornerstone of collective security in the twenty-first century."[8]

In June 2001 Annan released an ambitious report called "Prevention of Armed Conflict." He wrote that since assuming office he had endeavored to move the United Nations from a culture of reaction to a "culture of prevention," adding that it was time "to translate the rhetoric of conflict prevention into concrete action." He noted that the UN Charter placed the primary responsibility for conflict prevention with national governments, aided by civil society. The United Nations and the international community were expected to support national efforts for conflict prevention. Annan acknowledged that prevention is difficult. "Existing problems usually take precedence over potential ones, and while the benefits of prevention lie in the future and are difficult to quantify, the costs must be paid in the present."[9]

In his final year as secretary-general, Annan released a progress report on prevention. "A culture of prevention is beginning to take hold at the United Nations, and considerable progress has been made at both the international and national levels, with new tools and mechanisms being developed all the time," he said. But he acknowledged "an unacceptable gap remains, however, between rhetoric and reality. Too often the international community spends vast sums of money to fight fires that, in hindsight, we might have easily extinguished with timely preventive action before so many lives were lost or turned upside down."[10]

Annan's successor, Ban Ki-moon, spoke often about prevention. His team developed the UN's Conflict Prevention Toolkit. It assigned special envoys to study territorial disputes and constitutional and electoral crises; and created special political missions that worked on elections, women's empowerment, and human rights; peacekeeping operations that brought military and police operations to work with civilian peacekeepers; and rapidly deployable mediation experts on peace talks, constitution drafting, and power sharing. Ban said the UN had played an important preventive role in defusing conflicts in Burkina Faso, Colombia, Kyrgyzstan, Guyana, and Liberia.[11]

Ban's successor, António Guterres, also insisted that prevention was vital. At his first Security Council session in 2017, he said the United Nations was established to prevent war, but it now spent more time and resources responding to crises. "We need a whole new approach," he declared. "It has proved very difficult to persuade decision-makers at national and international levels that prevention must be their priority—perhaps because successful prevention does not attract attention. The television cameras are not there when a crisis is avoided," he said. Guterres said that global diplomacy has been dominated by responding to conflict but needed to do more to prevent war and sustain peace.

"Prevention is not merely a priority, but *the* priority. If we live up to our responsibilities we will save lives, reduce suffering, and give hope to millions," he said.[12]

Later that year Guterres again emphasized the issue. "Prevention should permeate everything we do. It should cut across all pillars of the UN's work and unite us for more effective delivery. We cannot meet the prevention challenge with the status quo. The United Nations needs to be much more unified in its thinking and in its action and put people at the center of its work."[13]

He has continued to speak about the need for prevention during his time as secretary-general.

THE PROBLEM OF PREVENTION

The idea of a culture of prevention has been part of the diplomatic discourse for the last several decades. It has been championed by respected diplomats, such as Eliasson, and has been broadly accepted and embraced by UN leaders. Few dispute that a culture of prevention is an excellent idea in concept, but analysts warn of its complications.

British diplomat Robert Cooper has argued that while conflict prevention is a compelling theory, it is hard to implement, especially when the primary source of conflict is within states. Cooper says although the case for stopping conflicts before they start is persuasive, practical obstacles often intrude. "The difficulty with preventing conflicts is not that they are unexpected. Provided governments are reasonably alert, the signs of a coming conflict are almost always there to see. This is true both over the months, sometimes years, when tensions build up, and also in the frantic period when conflict has begun to seem inevitable. No civil crisis is unpredicted. The difficulties for concerned countries are in deciding to act, and then in finding the right action." Cooper notes that often a country at risk will have lived for years with tension between certain groups. Other times there have been false alarms—when tensions rose sharply but major bloodshed was avoided. Even if one can see a conflict coming, it is difficult to guess exactly when and how it may break out. "Even when a crisis is predictable you still have to take decisions at short notice and act quickly—which is not easy. And the action will probably not be cheap," Cooper says. He adds that interventions are both risky and expensive and that few publics will applaud leaders who spend taxpayer dollars on "something which may not happen, and which is not your problem anyway. Besides, the local people, whose problem it is, understand it much better and will be better equipped to solve it."

He argues that there is little political pressure, encouragement, or reward to intervene early. "Doing nothing is always the easiest course—and much of the time it will seem to be a successful strategy. The obstacles to preventative intervention are therefore many and serious. There are not many cases where international intervention has prevented a conflict."[14]

Australian scholar Alex Bellamy shares Cooper's cautionary views. He argues that conflict prevention requires costs before the outbreak of violence and gives political leaders no way of proving that the commitment of resources yields the desired result. "In other words, conflict prevention requires governments to ask their citizens to commit resources to regions not yet in conflict, and if violence is averted, leaves them open to the accusation that they have wasted precious tax monies averting nonexistent conflicts. As Rwanda and Darfur show only too well, it is difficult enough to secure the political will necessary for a serious commitment in halting genocide and mass killing once they are under way." He adds that it's usually difficult to discern what steps might be useful and what entity should take the lead. Where does the responsibility to protect reside—with global powers, regional powers, regional organizations, or the UN? The central challenge of prevention, Bellamy argues, is that it is "an inherently speculative domain."[15]

ELIASSON CONTINUES TO CALL FOR PREVENTION

Eliasson understands the challenges of creating a culture of prevention and especially making it work in real time. Yet he remains convinced that it is essential and has not given up on his quest. Eliasson's focus and belief is grounded in both the ideals of Swedish foreign policy and his personal experiences. He has seen war zones and refugee camps—and the memories still haunt him.

Given his background as a mediator and a diplomat, Eliasson is especially committed to what has been called direct measures, or operational prevention, to stop conflicts from turning violent or recurring. He has even delved into the discipline of psychology to better understand why leaders and publics find it so difficult to act to forestall disasters. "Why is evidence of an approaching conflict and an impending human catastrophe often rejected? Why are we not prepared to see the writing on the wall before humanitarian action turns into a major military operation?" he wonders.

He is convinced that the conceptual framework that he and Wallensteen developed more than a quarter-century ago still provides a practical road map for policymakers.

Eliasson's passion for prevention began during his days as a Swedish diplomat and continued as he assumed high-level positions in the UN. During his presidency of the UN General Assembly, Eliasson spoke often of prevention. "The nightmare of Somalia in 1992–93 will forever remind me of the urgent need for prevention, for action for effectively dealing with civil wars, and the tormenting ethnic and religious conflicts. We cannot, after Cambodia, Rwanda, Srebrenica, and Darfur, continue to say, 'never again' without seriously undermining the moral authority of the UN and its charter," he said.[16] As deputy secretary-general he spoke frequently of prevention. Early in his tenure he said, "We hardly ever hear about successful conflict prevention, because violent conflict defused by diplomacy is often not considered as newsworthy. Have you ever seen headlines in the press saying a disaster did not occur? During my time as minister of foreign affairs of Sweden I worked intensely to put conflict prevention on the international agenda. But I found that it was difficult to get support for preventive measures because people don't want to deal with something that is not an immediate danger. We are stuck in the short term. Unfortunately, we don't often hear of many examples of successful crisis prevention, but there are a few. Ultimately, effective prevention is about picking up the early signs of conflicts before the situation escalates." In one of his final interviews as deputy secretary-general, he lamented the tendency to "get interested in a wound only when it is infected."

Eliasson, now in private life in Sweden, says he has never been more convinced of the necessity of creating a culture of prevention. "I'm obsessed with this idea." He argues that prevention is not an aspiration but a responsibility built into the UN Charter, specifically in Article 1, Article 33, and Article 99.[17]

However, large questions remain. Is a culture of prevention possible? Is it a poetic ideal or a real-world aspiration? How can it be operationalized in our complex international landscape with 193 independent nations? Should the UN be the lead actor, especially with the frequently divided Security Council? Will nations ever take hard actions, including allocating resources, to prevent crises in faraway lands?

PART IV

LESSONS LEARNED

CHAPTER 8

The Sage of Stockholm

LEAVING NEW YORK

In 2016, as he approached the final weeks of his service as the UN deputy secretary-general, Jan Eliasson braced for a potentially wrenching transition to private life. He was departing the United Nations and New York and ending his career as a full-time diplomat. In both a practical and symbolic way, he would soon be holding a one-way plane ticket to Stockholm.

In interviews before his departure, Eliasson was subdued, wistful, and reflective. He worried about pressing global challenges and pondered the end of his remarkable diplomatic career. He had relished his late career surge, with surprising opportunities in the last decade that included service as president of the UN General Assembly, Sweden's foreign minister, UN special envoy to Darfur, culminating as the deputy secretary-general. At the age of seventy-six he was aware that, while there would be special projects ahead, his status as a full-time Swedish or international diplomat was drawing to a close. "Now it's really final," he said.

Eliasson was deeply unsettled by the United States' recent election of Donald Trump, stunned that a country he knew so well and loved so deeply was poised to take such a perilous turn. He was apprehensive about what this might portend for the rules-based international order that he believed in so strongly and worked so hard for half a century to build and maintain. Eliasson was proud of his work at the UN and appreciative of his rich and multifaceted career. He called it a wonderful journey and felt intense gratitude. He reflected on his parents and the pride they would have felt at his accomplishments.

His final days at the UN were poignant, melancholy, and bittersweet. He knew he would miss the vitality and richness of New York City and the fascination and consequence of international diplomacy. As he prepared to leave, he packed up his apartment and organized his files. There were parties and receptions to attend and phone calls to colleagues, expressing appreciation and vowing to keep in touch. Ban Ki-moon, the secretary-general, held a special reception for him at UN headquarters that featured a self-effacing video spoof by Ban and warm toasts.

On his final day, as he prepared to leave for the airport, Eliasson said an emotional farewell to his staff and was met at the elevator on the 38th floor by the secretary-general, who rode down with him to the lobby. As Eliasson prepared to walk out of the UN building and into a waiting limousine, he was greeted by dozens of diplomats waving copies of his beloved UN Charter, thus providing the best possible tribute to the departing diplomat. He was driven by UN security to the airport and ushered to his first-class seat, where he chatted with flight attendants before settling in with a newspaper for the long flight across the Atlantic Ocean.

Hours later, at the arrivals gate at the Stockholm airport, Eliasson pushed a cart with several pieces of luggage, looking like a regular holiday traveler. He was eager to enjoy Christmas with his family but also uncertain about his future. He acknowledged that his hectic diplomatic life had been "a little bit like a drug" and he was not sure how he would react to withdrawal. He vowed to take several months off before considering offers. He wanted to read, relax, decompress, and think. He was open to new projects but wanted them to be interesting, stimulating, and consequential.

STOCKHOLM INTERNATIONAL PEACE RESEARCH INSTITUTE

Several months after returning to Stockholm, Eliasson accepted an offer to chair the Stockholm International Peace Research Institute. SIPRI is a prestigious think tank created by the Swedish government in 1966 to conduct research on peace and security. It publishes careful reports and trusted reference guides, including the annual SIPRI Yearbook on arms control, disarmament, and international security.

The chairmanship of SIPRI was an excellent platform for Eliasson to stay connected to global leaders and international issues. He used the position to think about a broader definition of security, one that went beyond the military and armaments. He believed security needed to include climate, public health, and natural disaster response policies. SIPRI's research program delved deeply into these issues and also advocated that the UN Security Council and the Swedish government consider the many security dimensions of climate-related disasters.

Eliasson enjoyed working with SIPRI's international board of directors and added several members with whom he had worked in the past, including Jessica Matthews from the United States, Jean-Marie Guehenno from France, and Chan Heng Chee from Singapore. Eliasson served as chair for five years and then became an associate fellow at SIPRI.[1]

THE SUMMIT

In 2017 Eliasson was invited by FLX, a Swedish production company, to host a series of televised conversations with global leaders called "The Summit." He worked with a team of producers to find compelling guests and prepare for substantive discussions. He traveled to interview former US secretary of state Madeleine Albright in Washington, former UN secretary-general Kofi Annan in Geneva, former Norwegian prime minister Gro Harlem Brundtland in Oslo, and former US secretary of state and national security advisor Henry Kissinger in New York.

The four episodes aired that fall and feature Eliasson interacting on equal footing with diplomatic luminaries. The discussions were friendly, respectful, and substantive. Eliasson steered the conversations to the background of the guest, but also invited each to discuss the issues of the day and some broader themes. He frequently brought up the notion of a "dialogue deficit" and "diplomacy deficit." The conversations with Albright, Annan, and Brundtland were relaxed and informal; they were all old friends. His interview with Kissinger was more formal and included a discussion of Sweden's clash with the United States in the 1970s over the Vietnam War. Kissinger was then the national security advisor and secretary of state in the Nixon administration and Eliasson was a junior aide to the Swedish prime minster, Olof Palme, a chief critic of American policy. The televised exchange between Eliasson and Kissinger was cordial and softened palpably when Eliasson handed Kissinger a photo of a meeting between Kissinger and Palme, with a youthful Eliasson looking on in the background. "We are having this interview because of my deep respect for you," Kissinger told Eliasson.[2]

MINISTERS FORUM

Eliasson also participates in the Aspen Institute's Ministers Forum that was established by Albright in 2003. Though Eliasson was Sweden's foreign minister for only six months, he still gained entry into this prestigious group that met once or twice a year. The forum provides former global leaders opportunities to relive a bit of the past, discuss current and future challenges, and issue statements and studies to shape current policy debate.

In June 2020 Eliasson added his signature to the forum's hard-hitting statement during the Covid-19 crisis, urging greater global cooperation and a renewed commitment to multilateralism. "Never before have we seen a challenge as acute, complex, far-reaching and potentially long-lasting as the Covid-19 pandemic," the statement said. "As with many of the threats we face, the virus does not respect boundaries and therefore cannot be defeated by any country acting alone." It added that the former leaders had all experienced the benefits that cooperative action can bring and hoped to encourage partnerships between local, national, regional, and global institutions that the crisis required. Vigorous multilateral measures can complement steps by national governments, rather than undermine them. They said the UN should take a more active role in responding to the public health crisis. The forum urged the General Assembly to hold an emergency summit and the Security Council to convene global institutions to devise an economic recovery plan and a coordinated debt relief plan. They urged national leaders and governments to increase funding for international organizations working on the pandemic, commit to equitable distribution of the vaccine, expand protections for women, support rigorous science, and promote cooperative action. The statement ended with a dig saying that current global leadership "is damaging and what the world is experiencing now must not happen again." With this statement, Eliasson and the Ministers Forum emphasized the essential need for strong multilateral institutions and global cooperation.[3] The forum, with Eliasson in attendance, convened in Prague in December 2022 to discuss democracy promotion, and in Copenhagen in October 2023 to consider global regulation of artificial intelligence. He believes the group offers vast experience and a useful perspective on global affairs.

GLOBAL LEADERSHIP PRIZE

While still at the UN, Eliasson was honored to learn that the prominent Tällberg Foundation was naming a prestigious leadership prize after him, describing him as "one of the most accomplished diplomats of our era." The international prize is given annually to leaders whose work is innovative, courageous, creative, and "rooted in universal values and global in implication." The prize was renamed the Tällberg-SNF-Eliasson Global Leadership Prize in 2017.[4] Several winners are chosen each year, all of whom have records of accomplishment and are likely to "continue to make extraordinary contributions to human welfare." The Tällberg Foundation seeks to establish a network of global leaders to tackle the most perplexing problems facing the international community. Eliasson is delighted to participate in events related to this prize.

EXPLAINING THE WORLD, CHALLENGING SWEDEN

Eliasson is frequently invited to discuss global and domestic affairs by Swedish organizations and media. He is an informed, polished, and effective commentator. He continues to study international affairs closely and still reads the *UN News Digest* daily. He can discuss global events easily and fluidly including, developments in the United States.

He has also discussed the large and consequential political changes occurring in Sweden as that nation, which has long been a progressive bastion, has turned to the right. The long-dominant Social Democratic Party, which Eliasson has supported since he was a young man, has suffered a decline of support from its commanding position half a century ago. The Social Democrats, considered a "left of center" party, have lost voters on the left to both the Greens and the Left Party, as well as on the right to mainstream conservative parties and, more alarmingly, to the Sweden Democrats, a right-wing nationalist party that embraces the mottos "Make Sweden Great Again" and "We say what you think."

Eliasson is troubled by the rise of the anti-immigrant, anti-Europe Sweden Democrats. He is concerned that Sweden, which for so long welcomed immigrants, now views them with hostility and suspicion. He acknowledges that Europe's and Sweden's political realities changed dramatically in the aftermath of the 2015 refugee crisis, when more than a million people fled turmoil in Iraq, Afghanistan, and Syria for Europe. Germany and Sweden accepted large refugee populations but have struggled to integrate them into their nations. This has led to a political and cultural backlash in both countries. Sweden has turned inward in response to globalization, immigration, and perceived threats to its national and cultural identity.

Eliasson argues that refugees and immigrants should be seen as human beings in need and as potential assets to host countries. However, this message is greeted skeptically in many parts of Sweden and Europe. Eliasson responds to this skepticism by focusing on themes he has long embraced: that immigrants bring energy, skills, and diversity to their new countries and there is an urgent need for governments to provide adequate housing, education, and employment for all their residents. He says another reason for domestic discontent is the widespread feeling that the government is not providing competent services and support.

Eliasson supported Sweden's decision to join NATO in the aftermath of Russia's invasion of Ukraine. Sweden applied for NATO membership in May 2022. In seeking to join the alliance, Sweden was prepared to give up two hundred years of military nonalignment. It had already deepened its cooperation with NATO in 2014 after Russia invaded eastern Ukraine and illegally annexed Crimea. Eliasson reflected long and hard before deciding to support this fundamental shift in Sweden's security policy. He was convinced that the Russian invasion of Ukraine fundamentally changed his nation's security calculations.

Eliasson has a following of 43,000 on X, formerly known as Twitter, and uses it to opine on the issues of the day, sometimes through the device of an ongoing conversation with his dog, Leo. Eliasson's posts are measured, but he is also willing to challenge and engage. "Sometimes I can't resist. I must show my colors. We have to sound the alarm." Eliasson frequently warns that democracy is under siege, the multilateral system is under threat, the migration and refugee challenge in Sweden must be dealt with humanely and competently, urgent action is needed to confront climate change and develop sustainable policies, and international cooperation is imperative.

He accepts offers from Sweden's foreign ministry and universities to speak to young diplomats and students about mediation, negotiation, and diplomacy. Eliasson's lectures are full of anecdotes and lessons from his illustrious career. He is convinced that stories and examples are the most effective way to communicate.

Eliasson enjoys his status as a major figure in Sweden and an international statesman. He maintains a respectful rivalry with Carl Bildt, his contemporary who was Sweden's prime minister from 1991 to 1994 and then served as foreign minister from 2006 to 2014. The two men occasionally appear together to discuss, and sometimes debate, current issues. Bildt, a conservative, is largely focused on national and European issues while Eliasson speaks often on global issues and the UN. They are often in agreement on foreign policy but occasionally take gentle jabs at each other on domestic matters.

Eliasson's 2022 memoir, *Word and Action*, was published in Swedish. He wrote it by hand and his wife, Kerstin, typed it. While his initial intention was to write a primer on diplomacy, the book became more of a personal story focusing on the people and experiences that shaped his life. It has been received warmly in Sweden, generating robust book sales and considerable attention.

He keeps in touch with former colleagues and mentees both in Stockholm and at the UN. Eliasson relishes the success of those he worked with. "Maybe the most important thing I can do now is pass on as much as possible to the next generation of diplomats. I believe in my profession. I've learned something about diplomacy during my years. It's important to convey as much as possible, and as generously as possible, to those who will drive Swedish foreign policy forward in the future and who will help shape the EU and the UN. It is important to hand over the baton."

When he's not lecturing, writing, or discussing global events, he plays tennis, swims, and walks. He and Kerstin frequently visit their farm in Gotland on the Baltic Sea. "It has been a fantastic life. I am very grateful."

CHAPTER 9

Statesmanship

TELLING THE TRUTH, OFFERING HOPE

As Jan Eliasson approached the end of his official diplomatic career, he understood that the global landscape was turning darker and more ominous. Hope and optimism seemed to be in retreat, and fear and anger were on the rise.

At an event in Washington, DC, in mid-November 2016, Eliasson demonstrated that statesmanship requires telling hard and challenging truths while also offering hope and solutions.

The occasion was a seminar sponsored by the Carnegie Endowment for International Peace. Friends, former colleagues, and his daughter, Anna, were in attendance. The mood was bittersweet. He was back with friends in a city he loves, but his more than forty-year career was winding down. Moreover, just two weeks earlier Eliasson's long commitment to multilateralism and global cooperation was dealt a crushing blow by the election of Donald Trump as president of the United States. Trump's "America First" campaign was based on views that Eliasson found flawed, foolish, and destructive.

Eliasson received a warm introduction by the president of the Carnegie Endowment, William Burns, a former American diplomat whose pedigree and reputation are commensurate with Eliasson's. Burns described Eliasson as "an extraordinary statesman" who has left "an important mark as a peacemaker." He praised Eliasson's "skills, savvy, and leadership," and said that he was "cast in the mold of the great line of

Swedish diplomats running from Raoul Wallenberg through Dag Hammarskjöld and Olof Palme. He has honored and built on their legacy." Burns described Eliasson as competent and bold. "No one has accused Jan of playing it safe. He is a person of action who is never afraid to be caught trying to do the right thing. In that way, he represents diplomacy and the United Nations at their very best."[1]

Eliasson walked to the podium, confident but also sober, even somber. He thanked Burns for his generous welcoming remarks and recalled their work "on so many barricades together over the years." Eliasson indirectly acknowledged the elephant in the room—the recent election of Trump—but did so within the strictures of diplomacy and protocol. He said he has "followed, almost too passionately, American political life" over the decades and confessed that he now feels "more uncertainty than I have felt in the past." He noted the "shaky ground on which we stand today" and referred to the "distinctly different climate now."

The diplomat then set aside his carefully prepared speech that was vetted by the UN bureaucracy. Eliasson had learned not to be indiscreet or publicly provocative. However, he felt compelled to address the moment now gripping the United States and the world. He also felt obligated to try to understand what led to Trump's election—and to frame it in global terms. There is, he observed, a growing tension between liberal internationalism, with its array of global institutions and agreements, and surging, even raging, populist nationalism in the United States, Europe, and elsewhere. Eliasson asserted that globalization "is still a very positive phenomenon" but its benefits have been unevenly distributed and are not evident to hundreds of millions of angry and frightened voters around the world. People are bewildered by "the speed of change," believe global elites have rigged the system, and are furious at the growing inequality within nations.

Turning to the institution he knows best, the United Nations, Eliasson saw a complex balance sheet with striking accomplishments and disappointing failures. It helped prevent another world war and oversaw the decolonization of Asia and Africa after World War II. However, it has failed in several areas, most recently and spectacularly in Syria and Darfur. Going forward, the UN, he declared, must play a constructive role in improving life for the people of the world. "Our job is to reduce the gap between the world as it is and the world as it should be. We have to deliver. We have to connect. We have to be very practical. We have to be very hands-on. We have to make life better." Eliasson argued that global leaders must reestablish their credibility. "We need to restore faith in institutions and demand that institutions deliver. This is a time for soul searching, but also for innovative, hopeful action, and also realism. We simply have to deliver and connect and communicate. We have to prove that liberal internationalism is the best way to go."

He implored that this not be a time of despair but of renewed commitment. The forces of hope, optimism, and tolerance can still prevail.

DIPLOMACY AND STATESMANSHIP

Many diplomats are inclined to downplay the power of their profession or, at least, are more comfortable expressing its limitations. Burns, the accomplished American diplomat who was to serve as the director of the CIA, writes that diplomacy is "among the oldest professions, but is also among the most misunderstood, and the most unsatisfying to describe. It is by nature an unheroic, quiet endeavor, less swaggering than unrelenting, often unfolding in back channels out of sight and out of mind. Its successes are rarely celebrated, its failures almost always scrutinized." Diplomacy is about quiet power, the unglamorous work of preserving alliances, easing disputes, and making long-term investments in relationships. "Diplomacy is punctuated only rarely by grand public breakthroughs. Its benefits are hard to appreciate. Crises averted are less captivating than military victories."[2]

Eliasson is keenly aware of the limitations and constraints of diplomacy but celebrates its noble aspirations and its possibilities to do good. He believes it is an honorable, creative, and civilized profession that offers unique opportunities to prevent problems, find compromises, and save lives.

Not all diplomats are statesmen and not all statesmen are diplomats. Statesmanship can occur in other professions including politics, government, business, academics, and religion. This book has sought to show how diplomacy and statesmanship came together in the career of Jan

Eliasson. We have considered his background and examined in detail several examples of his diplomatic work. We will now widen our lens to reflect on the aspects of his work that earn him the designation of statesman.

DEFINING STATESMANSHIP

At least since the times of Aristotle and Plato, political thinkers have tried to discern and describe the essential elements of statesmanship. The discussion has ranged from the numbingly esoteric to the deeply practical. For our purposes let's define statesmanship as exceptional leadership that is visionary, courageous, compassionate, effective, inspirational, and resilient.

Vision

Eliasson never had a Kissinger-like approach to diplomacy. He does not see the world as a complex chessboard in which leaders with sweeping grand strategies maneuver, duel, and remake the world. Eliasson is interested in diplomatic history but has little interest in diplomatic theory. He remains a student of diplomacy, but, more than anything, he has been a practitioner. He sees the world as a complex amalgam of countries, institutions, challenges, and people whose specific histories must be acknowledged and respected.

Eliasson's vision of international affairs is animated by his reverence for the rules-based order that was created after 1945. This system, he contends, provides security, prosperity, and stability, and champions human rights. It is a system based on the enlightened self-interest of all nations in which adherence to internationally negotiated rules and procedures demands some sacrifices by all, to achieve a greater good. Eliasson is convinced the UN should be at the heart of this rules-based order but acknowledges the importance of other organizations, including the World Bank, International Monetary Fund, World Trade Organization, NATO, and regional entities such as the European Union, the Organisation for Economic Co-operation and Development, the African Union, and others.

Eliasson openly acknowledges that the UN is a flawed institution that has not always lived up to its values. However, he emphasizes it is the only global body in which representatives from all countries can discuss challenges and opportunities and attempt to chart a common course. He argues passionately that the UN Charter and the Universal Declaration of Human Rights are landmark documents that can guide us to a better world. He frequently says that if the UN were shuttered, a similar organization would have to take its place and the result would likely be less successful than what was created in San Francisco in 1945.

Eliasson's conviction about the need for a culture of prevention is an essential component of his overall vision. A focus on prevention should be based on the premise that many conflicts and problems are not only foreseeable but are foreseen. However, political leaders and institutions tend to be reactive, only responding to crises rather than preempting them. He has advocated for this culture of prevention for decades and has even studied how diplomacy and psychology might collaborate to foster it.

Courage

Eliasson has demonstrated considerable physical and moral courage throughout his diplomatic career that has taken him into war zones and refugee camps in Africa, the Middle East, and the Balkans. He has worked amidst real personal threats. However, even when he was forced to leave a region for his own safety, he always returned to offer succor and solutions.

He has also displayed courage in the corridors of the UN and at diplomatic conferences. He has risked professional criticism by advancing policies that departed from the prevailing consensus. During his time as president of the UN General Assembly, he battled John Bolton, the American ambassador to the UN. While this made him popular at the UN, it complicated his relationship with the Bush administration and senior American officials who were important to his international success. As the UN deputy secretary-general he clashed with senior members of the Secretariat over the Human Rights Up Front program and strongly pushed for a UN apology for its role in accidentally bringing cholera to Haiti. He was willing to be a minority voice in meetings, challenging courses of action that he felt were misguided. The courage of the conference room should not be minimized. One colleague who watched him wage these intra-UN battles said he represented "the very best of the UN, as a voice of principle, as a force for good."

Eliasson does not enjoy conflict, but he is willing to act forcefully when needed to advance an important issue or cause. He never sought fights but neither did he avoid them. He can be tough and relentless; he believes effective diplomacy includes being willing to disagree and state those disagreements clearly.

Compassion

The enormous suffering Eliasson witnessed around the world has touched him deeply. He often recalls his heartbreaking work as the UN under-secretary-general for humanitarian affairs. The sight of dying children in Somalia and Darfur still haunts him, decades later. Tellingly, he responded to those tragedies by renewed resolve rather than falling into the paralysis of anguish. His compassion is evident by his personal conduct throughout his career. He treats people with respect and empathy, a habit he traces to his working-class roots. "He was the busiest man in the building, but he saw everyone. He always had time for everyone," an aide said about his time as deputy secretary-general. Throughout his career, Eliasson has emphasized the need to blend passion and drive with kindness and empathy.

Effective

Eliasson is a problem solver who insists on competence, though he prefers perfection. He spent his career fighting to make organizations work better and people's lives more secure. Eliasson is skillful at analyzing information, listening, developing formulations to explain problems, identifying solutions, and inspiring action. He encourages students and young colleagues to develop roots and wings—to cherish their personal histories but to be willing to leave home and learn about new worlds. He developed an easy-to-digest primer on negotiating that focuses on careful use of language, timing, cultural sensitivity, and personal relationships.

It has been said that diplomacy is primarily about language and people, and Eliasson has a facility for both. In addition to his native Swedish, he speaks fluent English, French, and German. And knows Latin, for good measure. He writes clearly and succinctly and is a skilled and exacting editor. His editing is especially ruthless when it comes to documents issued in his name. He urges young diplomats to become fluent in several languages, especially English, and to collect words and synonyms as essential tools of diplomacy. He recalls several episodes in his career in which the use of the right word or formulation paved the way for an agreement that saved lives. He contends that the use of the term "humanitarian corridor," rather than "ceasefire," broke a tense impasse in Sudan and ultimately saved thousands of lives.

Inspirational

Eliasson is a natural leader. He has an open and confident personality with a take-charge attitude that most find easy to work with. He naturally gravitates to the center of action and throughout his career was very often at the heart of the most important negotiations. He has never been one to hover on the periphery or wait hopefully or expectantly for an assignment. He volunteers for the big jobs. Eliasson's self-confidence and optimism are palpable and contagious.

He is at his best when leading a small team where his confidence and savvy are evident. He pushes people hard but also knows when to hold back and loosen up. "He had extremely high demands on his staff," said a former assistant. "He could be very tough. He is very detail oriented and a micromanager," said another aide.

He is a performer, an actor, and a storyteller. He understands that most people remember stories better than unadorned facts, hence his frequent aphorisms. "Jan is a combination of star diplomat and politician. That makes him unique. He has charisma. He can capture people's interests and capture their imagination. He engages with people," according to one aide. Throughout his career Eliasson was deeply ambitious but kept his ambitions under check. Photos from his younger days show a wiry and intense man, seemingly willing to elbow his way to advancement.

However, he mellowed over the years as he ascended the ranks of Swedish and global diplomacy.

Resilient

Eliasson enjoys the gift of resilience. That, combined with his energy and optimism, is a formidable combination for a diplomat. He is an intense man, but calm and controlled during crises. He does not allow his emotions to dominate his decision making. "He is not bothered easily by things," said one aide. "Jan never got jaded. He never gave up. He always said there is a way, a path to success. For Jan, there is always hope." He channels his emotional energy into finding solutions rather than agonizing about the past or lamenting current predicaments.

One of the keys to his resilience has been his ability to compartmentalize. He is capable of working long hours under difficult circumstances but adept at shutting down and getting eight hours of sleep a night. He has outlets to unwind—classical music, tennis, swimming, walking, and relaxing at his summer home in Gotland.

FOSTERING STATESMANSHIP

If the precise definition of statesmanship has been under discussion for millennia, so too has the question of how to mold or foster statesmanship. How do we create statesmen like Jan Eliasson? Of course, there is no exact formula; statesmen and stateswomen have come from a wide array of backgrounds. However, Eliasson's childhood and formative experiences are instructive.

Eliasson had remarkable parents—loving, supportive, demanding, and challenging. His father was stern and hard-driving, but also measured, fair, and honorable. His mother was deeply kind and nurturing. Eliasson's parents had a limited education—his father had seven years of school and his mother only four—yet they instilled in their children a reverence for education as a practical tool to operate and advance in the world and to make contributions to their communities. They had high expectations of their sons; they were implicit, unspoken, and clearly understood.

Eliasson's high school year in the United States was eye opening and life changing. His instinctive curiosity about the world expanded and his fascination with the United States became intense and lifelong. He learned he could adapt to new environments and excel. The Swedish Navy gave him a strong foundation. There he developed leadership skills, management experience, and national security credentials that he used throughout his career. Nautical references stayed with him throughout his life; he frequently characterized workplaces and organizations as happy, or unhappy, ships.

Eliasson was trained by one of the world's best foreign services. He developed deep and wide-ranging skills in analysis, negotiation, problem solving, and languages. He had several important mentors who were superb diplomats. They were deeply interested in him and invested in his success. They supported, challenged, and promoted him. Eliasson was a golden boy but was never pampered. He outworked most of his colleagues but wore his ambition lightly—most of the time—as he rose through the ranks. He had challenging professional opportunities in Stockholm, other European nations, the United States, and Africa. He learned the skills of both bilateral and multilateral diplomacy. And he developed an expertise in mediation that won him notice and praise, expanded his contacts, and advanced his career.

Just when it appeared that his career had reached its apex as Sweden's ambassador to the United States, and as semi-retirement beckoned, Eliasson was wise and ambitious enough to seize unanticipated opportunities at the UN and as Sweden's foreign minister. These experiences elevated him, broadened his worldview, and allowed him to continue his career as one of the great diplomats of his generation.

Through it all his supportive and accomplished wife, Kerstin, held the family together through numerous overseas moves. She has been kind, discrete, challenging, and a perfect sounding board. "Kerstin allowed him to have a family and also realize his ambitions. She centered him, anchored him," said a friend. So did his children.

Though Eliasson had what some may see as a charmed career, he also experienced setbacks and disappointments. The 1986 murder of Olof Palme was personally devastating and professionally unsettling. His difficult and contentious relationship with Secretary-General Boutros Boutros-Ghali during his time as under-secretary-general shook, but later fortified, him. His inability to broker a peace agreement in Darfur jolted him, but he channeled his disappointment into launching a clean water and sanitation initiative. In each case, he was able to pivot and move on.

Eliasson continued to grow, improve, deepen—and become ever more adept at blending the skills of statecraft, stagecraft, and soulcraft. He became a global statesman. So how can statesmanship, of the type Eliasson has displayed, help us confront the existential global challenges that are no longer at our doorstep but are breaking down the front door?

CHAPTER 10

Fixing the World

SYSTEM UNDER SIEGE

Jan Eliasson has observed and participated in a great deal of diplomatic history over the last fifty years. He has seen and experienced much that gives him hope and a lot that is dispiriting. As he studies the world now from his home in Stockholm, he acknowledges that he vacillates between being an "optimist who is worried" and a "pessimist who has not given up." He most often ends up on the side of guarded optimism.

There is broad agreement that the rules-based order of institutions and alliances created after World War II is eroding. Two schools of thought have emerged as to how global leaders should respond. Some posit that there is an urgent need for a "1945 moment" in which the entire multilateral system is overhauled. Others contend that there is simply no consensus on what a new system would look like and that the rivalry and antagonism between the United States and China as well as between the United States and Russia prevent any meaningful structural reforms. Additionally, with large existential problems threatening humanity's immediate future, there simply isn't time to launch a major reform process.

Eliasson is dismayed by the fraying of the international order and concludes that a fundamental overhaul is impractical because there is neither political consensus nor wide-ranging trust among the most powerful nations. He believes that institutions and governments must focus on delivering basic services and on explaining themselves to an angry, fearful, and skeptical public. Current multinational institutions and global alliances must be maintained, while their leaders need to look for adjustments and reforms at the margins. "We should not abandon the system that was created after 1945," Eliasson declares. "We should try to restore what we have. Any effort to create a new international system would fail because of the lack of trust."

Eliasson acknowledges that declining trust among national governments, international organizations, and the public is a stark reality that limits reform possibilities. Rebuilding this trust is imperative in order to diminish some of the fear that is sweeping the world. The UN Charter and the Universal Declaration of Human Rights, he believes, provide a solid foundation for the future. Nations need to listen to their people and focus on providing effective health care, education, employment, housing, and transportation. "We don't deliver well enough. We have to deliver."

While focusing on providing better governance, national leaders must emphasize and explain that a well-functioning global system serves *all* nations. Governments must embrace international cooperation as the basis to create a better future. "We live in a world of interdependence. We need to work together. The lines between national and international have been blurred. A well-functioning international system is good for all countries. We have to make international cooperation be seen as necessary and in the national interest," Eliasson argues.

He believes that leaders of national and global institutions must reach out to academic, nongovernmental, business, scientific, and other communities and find areas of collaboration and common purpose. "We need more stakeholders in individual countries and around the world. We have to establish the order on a broader basis."

RUSSIA'S INVASION OF UKRAINE

In Eliasson's view, Russia's 2022 invasion of Ukraine was a fundamental attack on the rules-based order, violating foundational norms of sovereignty and territorial integrity. He acknowledges that he initially saw the Russian troop buildup in late 2021 and early 2022 as a tactical move to wring concessions from Ukraine and NATO. He was stunned and dismayed by the invasion, feeling a "sense of emptiness and despair." He was encouraged by the strong support for Ukraine from Europe, the United States, and the West, and he supported the decision of the UN General Assembly to remove Russia from the Human Rights Council.

A lifelong proponent of diplomacy, Eliasson fears that it may be a long time before it is an effective instrument to end this war. The ambitions of Russia and Ukraine are now so fundamentally different that he believes a peace negotiation would be futile. Russian president Vladimir Putin seeks to reconstitute an assertive Russian empire while Ukraine wants to return to its 1991 borders that include Crimea. Eliasson is convinced political machinations and military developments will dominate the crisis for the foreseeable future. "I have difficulty finding a diplomatic way out. There are no prospects for a negotiation. The gap is too wide. For me as diplomat and peace negotiator this is painful to conclude. I hope a combination of political and military developments in due time will create a different diplomatic playing field."

The principle of respect for internationally recognized borders is the core of the rules-based order. Eliasson is convinced the West must continue to support Ukraine, financially, militarily, and politically, in defense of this principle.

UN REFORM

Eliasson has served in more high-level positions at the UN than anyone else in its history and has observed, and participated in, multiple attempts to reform the global body. He reviews reform proposals with interest but believes the current focus should be to make the current institutions in the UN system work better. "You have to be very tough and concrete." He is deeply disappointed in the Security Council's inability to constructively deal with major peace and security challenges. It has become paralyzed by disputes among its most powerful countries, the so-called Permanent Five—the United States, United Kingdom, France, Russia, and China—who have veto power and often use it to derail resolutions they don't like. The Security Council, Eliasson declares, should become a negotiating forum in which imperfect solutions are developed, rather than as a stage for all-or-nothing showdowns. It needs to become more like the Catholic

Church's College of Cardinals when they meet to elect a pope. "We need to see more deliberation and more white smoke," he quips.

He is frustrated and angry at the Security Council's lack of action to confront the wars in Syria, Yemen, Sudan, and Ukraine. This failure has undermined faith in the UN throughout the world, has led to the deaths of millions, and sent millions of refugees fleeing their homes in search of safety and hope.

The veto power held by the Security Council's Permanent Five is causing grave damage to the international order, but Eliasson does not see a scenario in which it is eliminated. Each of the Permanent Five would resist major change. "To me the veto is an admission of defeat. Casting the veto should be seen as a failure. It's hard to abolish it, but it must be seen as a failure." He envisions a major push to expand the Security Council to make it more representative of the twenty-first-century world.

If the Security Council remains stymied, it will become a less relevant body both in the UN and globally. Eliasson believes the UN General Assembly is poised to assume a larger role. It "should take advantage of this moment, this vacuum." In 2022 the General Assembly adopted a landmark resolution that stipulates that when a member of the Permanent Five vetoes a resolution, the matter is sent to the General Assembly for review and discussion.[1] While this procedure does not vitiate the veto, it allows a debate to go forward and puts pressure on the vetoer to explain its position. Eliasson would like the General Assembly to become the venue for wide-ranging policy debates and ultimately evolve into a global parliament.

He is convinced the UN secretary-general needs to play an assertive role on the global stage, offering moral, political, and diplomatic leadership. He or she should be willing to invoke Article 99, which states: "The Secretary-General may bring to the attention of the Security Council any matter which in his opinion may threaten the maintenance of international peace and security."[2] Article 99 has only been used a few times in UN history. Eliasson argues it should be used to trigger necessary debates even if members of the Permanent Five do not wish to engage in these discussions. He wonders if the invocation of Article 99 by the secretary-general before the Russian invasion of Ukraine in 2022 might have altered the calculations of the Russian leadership.

Eliasson believes the UN's most tangible contributions are in the field, conducting vital work in public health, poverty reduction, and humanitarian assistance. These programs cannot be taken for granted. They have saved millions of lives over the decades. They must be continued, strengthened, and publicly celebrated so people around the world are aware of the tangible benefits provided by the UN.

He has long argued that the UN needs to better integrate its peace and security, development, and human rights programs so these three areas are not cordoned off in institutional silos. Too often those working in security or in development do not believe their responsibilities extend into human rights. Eliasson is a strong proponent of multidisciplinary problem-solving teams. "We must think and act horizontally. We need to put problems at the center and focus on solving the problem rather than staying in our silos."

CLIMATE CHALLENGE

Eliasson believes that climate change and its related environmental challenges are the central issues of our time. The UN's commission of experts, the Intergovernmental Panel on Climate Change, reports that average global temperatures are expected to rise to 1.5 degrees Celsius (2.7 degrees Fahrenheit) above preindustrial levels by the first half of the 2030s. This would be massively disruptive, increasing the chances of extreme flooding, heat waves, drought, wildfires, and food shortages. The panel also reported that given current trends, temperatures could climb even higher, causing rising sea levels and massive global dislocation.[3]

"I cannot for my life understand why environmental issues have become a divisive political issue between the right and left of the political spectrum. Why are we so shortsighted? The destruction of our living conditions goes beyond right and left divisions. We are desperately in need of a unifying cause—within nations and in the international system. We need leadership to diminish the political battles on the environment," he said. "I hope to God we can leave this denial school behind us. If humanity is to have a long-term contract, we need to live with nature.

Over the years, we have robbed nature. Nature is in protest over what we are doing."

In December 2015, 196 global leaders signed the Paris Agreement on climate change. This treaty sets national targets for the world's nations to prevent global temperatures from rising to dangerous levels. Under the accords, for the first time almost every country in the world agreed to submit a voluntary plan to limit its carbon emissions.[4] Since then, the surge in global greenhouse gases has slowed, but not enough for the world to avoid major disruptions in the coming decades and beyond. Experts say that current climate pledges would put the planet on a path for about 2.5 degrees Celsius warming by 2100. This would have a calamitous impact for life on earth.

Eliasson has sympathy for those who call for a UN-sponsored global emergency declaration on climate. However, he fears that a protracted effort to negotiate such a declaration might degenerate into an international blame game and divert attention from the concrete policies needed if the Paris Climate Accords' goals are to be realized. "People desperately want this problem to be addressed and sometimes words can light up people. But I don't want to risk a diplomatic process that takes years, that distracts us, and exposes the divisions that are hurting us now." He believes the 17 Sustainable Development Goals, and especially their 169 subgoals, provide practical tools to address the climate crisis. "This is the action plan to achieve the Paris goals. We must change our way of thinking on climate. The SDGs are clear and concrete tools we can use."

PANDEMICS

There is, of course, no good time for a pandemic to spread across the world. But experts agree that the Covid-19 pandemic arrived at an especially unfortunate time in global affairs. China had grown combative and confrontational, the United States was erratic and dysfunctional, populist nationalists ruled in the United States, India, the United Kingdom, and Brazil, and basic science was under attack. Global cooperation collapsed into a state of recrimination and chaos. Virtually all key actors—the World Health Organization, the UN Security Council, China, the United States, and the European Union—failed to contain the disease, provide needed care to the sick, and fairly distribute vaccines. A distinguished group of experts, the Independent Panel for Pandemic Preparedness and Response, studied the global response and issued a scathing report. It concluded that most major institutions failed and there is an urgent need for a new global public health and emergency response that is "coordinated, connected, fast moving and accountable, just and equitable—in other words a complete pandemic preparedness and response system on which citizens can rely to keep them safe and healthy." Specifically, it called for a Pandemic Framework Treaty, a stronger and more credible WHO, and the creation of a Global Health Threats Council. Eliasson backs these ideas and emphasizes the need for early warning mechanisms.[5]

Eliasson laments the global response to the pandemic, saying it was more than disheartening—it was tragic. A renewed and tangible commitment to improve national and global public health systems and international cooperation is imperative. "The pandemic showed that we need to be much better prepared. We have to think in advance of worst-case scenarios and be prepared to move on the assumption they will occur. The Covid-19 crisis should be a wakeup call that we need to work cooperatively on climate and other global issues."

REFUGEE CRISES

Eliasson believes one of the central issues of the coming decades will be the growing numbers of refugees and migrants around the globe. Continuing wars in Ukraine, Syria, Yemen, and Sudan, and the likelihood of future wars, will shatter societies and send millions more fleeing for safety and support. Additionally, climate change will create its own refugee crisis. Some studies project that between 200 and 300 million people may become climate refugees in the coming decades as more areas of Africa and Asia become uninhabitable.

Eliasson recalls that the surge of refugees to Europe in 2015, due to wars in Syria, Afghanistan, Iraq, Libya, and elsewhere, "revolutionized" the political debate in Europe, giving far-right parties stronger electoral support for hardline anti-immigrant policies. According to the United Nations Refugee Agency's Global Report, there were nearly 12.4 million refugees in Europe by the end of 2022.[6] This transformed the politics in nations including Spain, Italy, Germany, and Sweden. These countries are still working to integrate refugees into their societies. Many European nations simply and firmly shut their borders to refugees. "Sadly, refugees and migrants are used as scapegoats for our problems. It's politically rewarding to blame refugees and migrants for everything that is wrong. This must stop. We have enough division and hatred in the world. We have to fight for human dignity, equality, and human rights," Eliasson says.

Eliasson ponders Europe's current struggles with its flood of millions of migrants as he tries to conceptualize the possibility of an influx of climate refugees. "Can you imagine the political effect of 200 to 300 million climate refugees? I fear it."

THE WAY AHEAD

The coming years will be extremely difficult. Leaders and publics will face the greatest array of complex problems and existential threats that humanity has ever confronted. UN Secretary-General António Guterres was not being hyperbolic when he said, "Our world has never been more threatened. Or more divided. We face the greatest cascade of crises in our lifetime."

Eliasson believes exceptional leadership, strong institutions, and engaged publics will be essential. Enlightened leaders working in creative and innovative problem-solving teams are imperative. Strong, resilient, and well-managed institutions must tackle hard challenges and solve problems before they become crises. Effective governance will be required to bolster publics that have grown wary, frightened, and fearful. Eliasson remains hopeful that extraordinary challenges will inspire visionary and competent leadership. True statesmanship will be needed at all levels of government and civic life.

The challenges ahead are daunting, and success is far from guaranteed. But instead of despair, let us remember these wise words of Jan Eliasson. "There is always a way. There is always hope. Giving up is unacceptable. It's undignified to give up."

NOTES

CHAPTER 1

1. Jan Eliasson, remarks to the UN General Assembly on the Draft Resolution of the Human Rights Council, March 15, 2006, https://www.un.org/en/ga/president/60/pdf/statements/20060315-hrc.pdf; "Assembly President Hails Vote on Human Rights Council as Marker of UN Reform," UN News, March 15, 2006, https://news.un.org/en/story/2006/03/172272. The UN issued a press release after the vote, https://press.un.org/en/2006/060315_eliasson_pc.doc.htm.

2. Jan Eliasson, "The Global Water and Sanitation Crisis," University of Gothenburg, TEDx Talks, December 2011, https://www.youtube.com/watch?v=8U-GaKqCzX4.

3. "Special Event Recital 'Markings and Music' Paying Tribute to Dag Hammarskjöld," United Nations, October 27, 2015, https://media.un.org/avlibrary/en/asset/d148/d1488319.

4. John F. Kennedy, State of the Union Address, January 30, 1961, National Archives, https://www.archives.gov/legislative/features/sotu/jfk.html.

CHAPTER 2

1. Olof Palme International Center, https://www.palmecenter.se/eng/about-palme-center/about-olof-palme.

2. "Wind and Sun," in *Aesop's Fables* (New York: Signet Classic, 1992), 98.

3. Jan Eliasson, remarks to the Swedish Parliament on the fiftieth anniversary of the disappearance of Raoul Wallenberg, January 17, 1995, International Raoul Wallenberg Foundation, https://www.raoulwallenberg.net/wallenberg/articles-47/speech-mr-jan-eliasson-swedish.

4. "Atlantic Storm," Johns Hopkins Bloomberg School of Public Health, table-top exercise, January 14, 2005, https://centerforhealthsecurity.org/our-work/tabletop-exercises/atlantic-storm-a-tabletop-exercise.

CHAPTER 3

1. UN Charter, https://www.un.org/en/about-us/un-charter.

2. Jan Eliasson, "The 2011 Dag Hammarskjöld Lecture," Dag Hammarskjöld Foundation, September 18, 2011, https://www.daghammarskjold.se/publication/dag-hammarskjold-lecture-2011.

3. Robert McFadden, "Brian Urquhart, Troubleshooter for the U.N., Dies at 101," *New York Times*, January 3, 2021, https://www.nytimes.com/2021/01/03/obituaries/brian-urquhart-dead.html.

4. Andrew Gilmour, "On the Death of a Diplomat: Brian Urquhart 1919–2021," *The Spectator*, January 4, 2021, https://www.spectator.co.uk/article/on-the-death-of-a-diplomat-brian-urquhart-1919-2021.

5. *The Economist*, "His UNdoing," December 7, 2006, https://www.economist.com/united-states/2006/12/07/his-undoing.

6. John Bolton, *Surrender Is Not an Option: Defending the United States at the UN* (New York: Simon & Schuster, 2007), 204.

7. United Nations Resolution, 46/182, https://undocs.org/Home/Mobile?FinalSymbol=A%2FRES%2F46%2F182&Language=E&DeviceType=Desktop&LangRequested=False.

8. Jan Eliasson, "Acceptance Speech of Mr. Jan Eliasson, President-elect of the 60th Session of the General Assembly," June 13, 2005, https://www.un.org/en/ga/president/60/pdf/statements/20050613-acceptancespeech.pdf; "General Assembly Elects Jan Eliasson of Sweden as President of Sixtieth Session," press release, June 13, 2005, https://press.un.org/en/2005/ga10355.doc.htm.

9. World Summit Outcome Document, September 16, 2005, https://www.un.org/en/genocideprevention/about-responsibility-to-protect.shtml.

10. Jan Eliasson, remarks to UN General Assembly at the conclusion of the sixtieth session, September 11, 2006, https://www.un.org/en/ga/president/60/pdf/statements/20060911-gadebateclosing.pdf.

11. "New Deputy Secretary-General to Focus on Development, Political Issues," *UN News*, July 19, 2012, https://news.un.org/en/story/2012/07/416002.

CHAPTER 4

1. Kofi Annan remarks to UN Human Rights Council, "UN Human Rights Council Commences First Session in Geneva," press release, June 19, 2006, https://www.ohchr.org/en/press-releases/2009/10/un-human-rights-council-commences-first-session-geneva.

2. Jan Eliasson remarks to UN Human Rights Council, "UN Human Rights Council Commences First Session in Geneva," press release, June 19, 2006, https://www.ohchr.org/en/press-releases/2009/10/un-human-rights-council-commences-first-session-geneva.

3. UN Charter, https://www.un.org/en/about-us/un-charter.

4. Andrew Clapham, *Human Rights: A Very Short Introduction* (Oxford: Oxford University Press, 2007), 49–54.

5. "A More Secure World: Our Shared Responsibility," Report of the High-level Panel on Threats, Challenges and Change, December 2, 2004, https://www.un.org/peacebuilding/content/more-secure-world-our-shared-responsibility-%E2%80%93-report-high-level-panel-threats-challenges-and.

6. Report of Secretary-General, "In Larger Freedom: Towards Development, Security, and Human Rights for All"; "Secretary-General Presents Report 'In Larger Freedom' to General Assembly, Outlining Ambitious Plan for United Nation Reform," press release, March 21, 2005, https://press.un.org/en/2005/ga10334.doc.htm.

7. UN General Assembly, "2005 World Summit Outcome," September 11, 2005, https://peacemaker.un.org/node/95.

8. Letter to Jan Eliasson from Amnesty International, Freedom House, World Federalist Movement, Refugees International and others, November 1, 2005. Joint Letter on the UN Human Rights Council, https://archive.globalpolicy.org/reform/topics/hrc/2005/1101joint.htm.

9. Jan Eliasson, "Statement of the President of the United Nations General Assembly . . . at the Informal Consultations of the Plenary on the Human Rights Council," February 23, 2006, https://www.ohchr.org/en/statements/2009/10/statement-president-united-nations-general-assembly-he-mr-jan-eliasson-informal.

10. Amnesty International Statement on Jan Eliasson proposal, February 23, 2006, https://archive.globalpolicy.org/reform/topics/hrc/2006/0223amnestyhrc.htm.

11. "The Shame of the United Nations," editorial, *New York Times*, February 26, 2006, https://www.nytimes.com/2006/02/26/opinion/the-shame-of-the-united-nations.html.

12. Mary Robinson, "Human Rights: A Needed UN Reform," editorial, *New York Times*, March 2, 2006, https://www.nytimes.com/2006/03/02/opinion/human-rights-a-needed-un-reform.html.

13. Jimmy Carter, Óscar Arias, Kim Dae Jung, Shirin Ebadi and Desmond Tutu, "Human Rights: Principles Defeat Politics at the UN," editorial, *New York Times*, March 5, 2006, https://www.nytimes.com/2006/03/05/opinion/05iht-edjimmy.html.

14. Jan Eliasson remarks to UN General Assembly, "Statement . . . on the Draft Resolution on the Human Rights Council," March 15, 2006, https://www.un.org/en/ga/president/60/pdf/statements/20060315-hrc.pdf.

15. John Bolton, "Remarks on the Draft Resolution for the Human Rights Council and Sudan," March 15, 2006, https://2001-2009.state.gov/p/io/rls/rm/62311.htm.

16. Ban Ki-moon, "Statement on the Internal Review Panel Report on Sri Lanka," November 14, 2012, https://www.un.org/sg/en/content/sg/speeches/2012-11-14/statement-internal-review-panel-report-sri-lanka.

17. "'Human Rights Up Front' Initiative," https://www.un.org/sg/en/content/human-rights-front-initiative.

18. Ban Ki-moon statement to UN Security Council, "Renewing Our Commitment to the Peoples and Purposes of the United Nations," November 22, 2013, https://www.un.org/sg/en/content/sg/speeches/2013-11-22/renewing-our-commitment-peoples-and-purposes-united-nations-scroll.

19. Jan Eliasson remarks to UN General Assembly, December 17, 2013, https://www.un.org/sg/en/content/deputy-secretary-general/statement/2013-12-17/deputy-secretary-generals-remarks-briefing-of-the-general-assembly-rights-front-prepared-for-delivery.

20. Jan Eliasson and Helen Clark letter to UN Resident Coordinators, February 24, 2014, in Ekkehard Strauss, "The UN Secretary-General's Human Rights Up Front

Initiative and the Prevention of Genocide: Impact, Potential, Limitations," *Genocide Studies and Prevention* 11, no. 3 (March 2018): 48–59, https://digitalcommons.usf.edu/cgi/viewcontent.cgi?article=1504&context=gsp.

21. Jan Eliasson comments, Human Rights up Front, An Overview, https://www.un.org/sg/en/content/human-rights-front-initiative.

22. Jan Eliasson remarks to UN General Assembly; "Prevention Fundamental Premise, Vocation Of Human Rights Up Front Initiative, Deputy Secretary-General Says at Dialogue with General Assembly," press release, January 27, 2016, https://press.un.org/en/2016/dsgsm931.doc.htm.

23. Kenneth Roth, "Why the UN Chief's Silence on Human Rights Is Deeply Troubling," *Washington Post*, April 25, 2019, https://www.hrw.org/news/2019/04/25/why-un-chiefs-silence-human-rights-deeply-troubling.

24. António Guterres, "The Highest Aspiration: A Call to Action for Human Rights," February 24, 2020, https://www.un.org/peacebuilding/sites/www.un.org.peacebuilding/files/documents/2020_sg_call_to_action_for_hr_the_highest_aspiration.pdf.

CHAPTER 5

1. Elizabeth Shackelford, *The Dissent Channel: American Diplomacy in a Dishonest Age* (New York: Public Affairs, 2020), 3–7.

2. Ban Ki-moon, *Resolved: Uniting Nations in a Divided World* (New York: Columbia University Press, 2021), 121.

3. Jan Egeland, *A Billion Lives: An Eyewitness Report from the Frontlines of Humanity* (New York: Simon & Schuster, 2008), 82.

4. Samantha Power, "Dying in Darfur," *New Yorker*, August 22, 2004, https://www.newyorker.com/magazine/2004/08/30/dying-in-darfur.

5. Abuja Peace Agreement; "Sudan Peace Agreement Signed 9 January Historic Opportunity, Security Council Told," press release, August 2, 2005, https://press.un.org/en/2005/sc8306.doc.htm.

6. "What Is R2P?," Global Centre for Responsibility to Protect, https://www.globalr2p.org/what-is-r2p.

7. "Former General Assembly President Chosen as UN Envoy for Darfur Crisis," *UN News*, December 19, 2006, https://news.un.org/en/story/2006/12/203892.

8. Jan Eliasson remarks at press conference in Sudan, January 11, 2007, https://reliefweb.int/report/sudan/sudan-near-verbatim-transcript-press-confrence-held-special-envoy-un-sgl-darfur-jan.

9. Jan Eliasson and Salim Salim joint press statement in Sudan, February 12, 2007, https://reliefweb.int/report/sudan/joint-press-statement-special-envoy-au-darfur-salim-ahmed-salim-and-un-sgs-special.

10. Walter Hoge, "Darfur Peace Talks in Danger of Lacking Attendance," *New York Times*, October 25, 2007, https://www.nytimes.com/2007/10/25/world/africa/25nations.html.

11. Jeffrey Gettleman, "Sudan Declares Darfur Cease-Fire," *New York Times*, October 28, 2007, https://www.nytimes.com/2007/10/28/world/africa/28iht-darfur.1.8079036.html.

12. Ban Ki-moon statement, delivered by Jan Eliasson, October 27, 2007, https://reliefweb.int/report/sudan/sudan-darfur-peace-talks-begin-secretary-general-commends-parties-making-choice.

13. Jan Eliasson remarks to UN Security Council, "Darfur: UN Envoy Doubtful Parties Are Willing to Enter Serious Negotiations," *UN News*, June 24, 2008, https://news.un.org/en/story/2008/06/264082-darfur-un-envoy-doubtful-parties-are-willing-enter-serious-negotiations.

14. Julie Flint, "Rhetoric and Reality: The Failure to Resolve the Darfur Conflict," HSBA Working Paper 19, *Small Arms Survey*, January 2010, https://www.smallarmssurvey.org/resource/rhetoric-and-reality-failure-resolve-darfur-conflict-hsba-working-paper-19.

CHAPTER 6

1. "All Eyes on UN as World Body Prepares to Adopt New Sustainable Development Goals," *UN News*, September 24, 2015, https://news.un.org/en/story/2015/09/509632.

2. "'The Future Demands of Us Critical and Global Decisions' Pope Francis Tells UN General Assembly," *UN News*, September 25, 2015, https://news.un.org/en/story/2015/09/509712.

3. Ban Ki-moon, "Remarks at Summit for the Adoption of the Post-2015 Development Agenda," September 25, 2015, https://www.un.org/sg/en/content/sg/speeches/2015-09-25/remarks-summit-adoption-post-2015-development-agenda.

4. Iris Borowy, "The Social Dimension of Sustainable Development at the UN: From Brundtland to the SDGs," April 2021, https://www.researchgate.net/publication/351175937_The_social_dimension_of_sustainable_development_at_the_UN_from_Brundtland_to_the_SDGs.

5. Millenium Development Goals, World Health Organization newsroom, February 19, 2018, https://www.who.int/news-room/fact-sheets/detail/millennium-development-goals-(mdgs).

6. Jeffrey Sachs, "From Millennium Development Goals to Sustainable Development Goals," *The Lancet* 379, no. 9832 (June 9, 2012): 2206–11, https://www.thelancet.com/journals/lancet/article/PIIS0140-6736%2812%2960685-0/fulltext.

7. Jan Eliasson, video testimonial for Millennium Development Goals, United Nations on YouTube, https://www.youtube.com/watch?v=6-6P3qFuHJk.

8. Report of the Secretary-General, "A Life of Dignity for All: Accelerating Progress Towards the Millennium Development Goals and Advancing The United Nations Development Agenda beyond 2015," July 26, 2013, https://sdgs.un.org/documents/a68202-life-dignity-all-accelerating-19856.

9. Jan Eliasson, press conference at UN, October 2, 2012, https://press.un.org/en/2012/dsgsm643.doc.htm.

10. Jan Eliasson, remarks at Friedrich Ebert Foundation, November 26, 2012, https://press.un.org/en/2012/dsgsm649.doc.htm.

11. Jan Eliasson, remarks, High Level Stocktaking Event on Post-2015 Development Agenda, September 11, 2014, https://www.un.org/sg/en/content/deputy-secretary-general/statement/2014-09-11/

deputy-secretary-generals-remarks-high-level-stocktaking-event-the-post-2015-development-agenda-prepared-for-delivery.

12. Jan Eliasson, remarks at the opening of the High-level Political Forum, July 6, 2015, https://sdgs.un.org/statements/mr-jan-eliasson-un-deputy-secretary-general-13755.

13. Jan Eliasson, remarks at the International Conference on Sustainable Development, September 24, 2015, https://press.un.org/en/2015/dsgsm894.doc.htm.

14. Barack Obama, "Remarks by President Obama to the United Nations General Assembly," September 28, 2015, https://obamawhitehouse.archives.gov/the-press-office/2015/09/28/remarks-president-Obama-united-nations-general-assembly.

15. Sustainable Development Goals, https://sdgs.un.org/goals.

16. *The Economist*, "The 169 Commandments," March 26, 2015, https://www.economist.com/leaders/2015/03/26/the-169-commandments.

17. William Easterly, "The SDGs Should Stand for Senseless, Dreamy and Garbled," *Foreign Policy*, September 28, 2015, https://foreignpolicy.com/2015/09/28/the-sdgs-are-utopian-and-worthless-mdgs-development-rise-of-the-rest.

18. Jan Eliasson remarks, Organisation for Economic Co-operation and Development, February 18, 2016, https://press.un.org/en/2016/dsgsm939.doc.htm.

19. Jan Eliasson remarks, UN General Assembly's High-level Political Forum, July 18, 2016, https://press.un.org/en/2016/ecosoc6785.doc.htm.

20. Frank Biermann, Thomas Hickmann, and Carole-Anne Sénit, eds., *The Political Impact of the Sustainable Development Goals: Transforming Governance through Global Goals?* (Cambridge: Cambridge University Press, 2022).

21. "The Sustainable Development Goals Report 2023: Special Edition," Department of Economic and Social Affairs, July 10, 2023, https://unstats.un.org/sdgs/report/2023.

22. UN Political Declaration, Sustainable Development Goals Summit 2023, September 18–19, 2023, New York, https://www.un.org/en/conferences/SDGSummit2023/political-declaration.

CHAPTER 7

1. Jan Eliasson, "A Culture of Prevention: Sweden and Conflict Prevention," in *Developing a Culture of Conflict Prevention* (Brussels: Madariaga European Foundation, 2004).

2. Sweden's Ministry of Foreign Affairs, "Preventing Violent Conflict: A Swedish Action Plan," January 1, 1999, https://www.government.se/legal-documents/1999/01/ds-199924.

3. Sweden's Ministry of Foreign Affairs, "Preventing Violent Conflict: Swedish Policy for the 21st Century," Government Communication, 2000, 2000/01:2.

4. "20th Anniversary of the EU Programme for the Prevention of Violent Conflict," EPLO blog, January 18, 2022, https://eploblog.wordpress.com/2022/01/18/20th-anniversary-of-the-eu-programme-for-the-prevention-of-violent-conflicts.

5. Olof Skoog, Concept Note, January 5, 2017, UN Security Council.

6. Margot Wallström, remarks to UN Security Council, January 10, 2017, https://www.un.org/sg/en/content/sg/secretary-generals-speeches?statID=574&page=121.

7. Report of the Secretary-General, "An Agenda for Peace: Preventive Diplomacy, Peacemaking and Peacekeeping," January 31, 1992, https://digitallibrary.un.org/record/144858?ln=en.

8. "Secretary-General Says Global Effort against Armed Conflict Needs Change from 'Culture of Reaction to Culture of Prevention,'" press release, November 29, 1999, https://press.un.org/en/1999/19991129.sc6759.doc.html.

9. "Annan Issues Far-Reaching Recommendations for Preventing Armed Conflict," *UN News*, June 15, 2001, https://news.un.org/en/story/2001/06/5462.

10. Report of the Secretary-General, "Progress Report on the Prevention of Armed Conflict," July 18, 2006, https://digitallibrary.un.org/record/581457/usage?ln=en.

11. Ban Ki-moon, "Preventive Diplomacy: Delivering Results," UNRCCA report, September 9, 2011, https://unrcca.unmissions.org/preventive-diplomacy-delivering-results-0.

12. "Secretary-General, in First Address to Security Council since Taking Office, Sets Restoring Trust, Preventing Crises as United Nations Priorities," press release, January 10, 2017, https://press.un.org/en/2017/sc12673.doc.htm.

13. António Guterres, remarks to the General Assembly, September 6, 2017, https://www.un.org/sg/en/content/sg/speeches/2017-09-06/secretary-generals-responsibility-protect-remarks.

14. Robert Cooper, "Notes on Conflict Prevention," in *Developing a Culture of Conflict Prevention* (Brussels: Madariaga European Foundation, 2004).

15. Alex Bellamy, "Mass Atrocities and Armed Conflict: Links, Distinctions, and Implications for the Responsibility to Prevent," Stanley Center for Peace and Security, February 2011, https://stanleycenter.org/publications/mass-atrocities-and-armed-conflict-links-distinctions-and-implications-for-the-responsibility-to-prevent.

16. Jan Eliasson, "Acceptance Speech of Mr. Jan Eliasson, President-elect of the 60th Session of the General Assembly," June 13, 2005, https://www.un.org/en/ga/president/60/pdf/statements/20050613-acceptancespeech.pdf; "General Assembly Elects Jan Eliasson of Sweden as President of Sixtieth Session," press release, June 13, 2005, https://press.un.org/en/2005/ga10355.doc.htm.

17. UN Charter, https://www.un.org/en/about-us/un-charter.

Chapter 8

1. Stockholm International Peace Research Institute, https://www.sipri.org.

2. "The Summit," Toppmötet, FLX Production Company, https://flx.se/project/toppmotet/.

3. Aspen Ministers Forum, "Twenty-Seven Foreign Ministers Issue Call for United Nations to Coordinate Global COVID-19 Response," June 12, 2020, https://www.aspeninstitute.org/of-interest/twenty-seven-foreign-ministers-issue-call-for-united-nations-to-coordinate-global-covid-19-response.

4. Tällberg-SNF-Eliasson Global Leadership Prize, https://tallberg-snf-eliasson-prize.org.

CHAPTER 9

1. "A Conversation with UN Deputy Secretary-General Jan Eliasson," Carnegie Endowment for International Peace, November 2016, https://www.youtube.com/watch?v=WbHPlgfjO2Y.

2. William Burns, *The Back Channel: A Memoir of American Diplomacy and the Case for Its Renewal* (New York: Random House, 2019), 10.

CHAPTER 10

1. "General Assembly Adopts Landmark Resolution Aimed at Holding Five Permanent Security Council Members Accountable for Use of Veto," GA/12417, press release, April 26, 2022, https://press.un.org/en/2022/ga12417.doc.htm.

2. UN Charter, Article 99, https://legal.un.org/repertory/art99.shtml.

3. Intergovernmental Panel on Climate Change, https://www.ipcc.ch/reports.

4. Paris Climate Agreement, UN Climate Change Conference, COP21, December 12, 2015, https://unfccc.int/process-and-meetings/the-paris-agreement.

5. Independent Panel for Pandemic Preparedness and Response, https://theindependentpanel.org.

6. UN Refugee Agency, Global Report 2022, https://www.unhcr.org/us/global-report.

Selected Readings

Madeleine Albright with Bill Woodward. *Hell and Other Destinations*. New York: HarperCollins, 2020.

Kofi Annan with Nader Mousavizadeh. *Interventions: A Life in War and Peace*. New York: Penguin Books, 2012.

Ban Ki-moon. *Resolved: Uniting Nations in a Divided World*. New York: Columbia University Press, 2021.

William Burns. *The Back Channel: A Memoir of American Diplomacy and the Case for Its Renewal*. New York: Random House, 2019.

Robert Cooper. *The Ambassadors: Thinking about Diplomacy from Machiavelli to Modern Times*. London: Weidenfield & Nicholson, 2021.

Gareth Evans. *Good International Citizenship: The Case for Decency*. Melbourne: Monash University Publishing, 2022.

Jussi Hanhimaki. *The United Nations: A Very Short Introduction*. Oxford: Oxford University Press, 2015.

Paul Kennedy. *The Parliament of Man: The Past, Present and Future of the United Nations*. New York: Random House, 2006.

Mark Malloch-Brown. *The Unfinished Global Revolution: The Pursuit of a New International Politics*. New York: Penguin Press, 2011.

George Packer. *Our Man: Richard Holbrooke and the End of the American Century*. New York: Alfred A. Knopf, 2019.

Samantha Power. *Chasing the Flame: One Man's Fight to Save the World*. New York: Penguin Books, 2008.

Samantha Power. *The Education of an Idealist: A Memoir*. New York: Dey Street Books, 2019.

John T. Shaw. *The Ambassador: Inside the Life of a Working Diplomat*. Potomac, MD: Capital Books, 2006.

James Traub. *The Best of Intentions: Kofi Annan and the UN in the Era of American Power*. New York: Picador, 2006.

Brian Urquhart. *A Life in Peace and War*. New York: W. W. Norton, 1987.

INDEX

About the Author

John T. Shaw's previous books include *Rising Star, Setting Sun: Dwight D. Eisenhower, John F. Kennedy, and the Presidential Transition That Changed America* (2018); *JFK in the Senate: Pathway to the Presidency* (2013); *Richard G. Lugar, Statesman of the Senate* (2012); *The Ambassador: Inside the Life of a Working Diplomat* (2006); and *Washington Diplomacy: Profiles of People of World Influence* (2002).

Shaw was a congressional and diplomatic correspondent in Washington, DC, for more than twenty-five years. He is director of the Paul Simon Public Policy Institute at Southern Illinois University. Shaw and his wife, Mindy, live in Carbondale, Illinois.